a devotiona

Mended
REMOVING THE BANDAGES

God Bless Glynn
Frebs
love you

Tamara Ellison

7/14/18

Tamara Ellison Ministries

8780 19th Street, Ste. #176

Alta Loma, CA 91701

Ordering Information:

For information about special discounts available for bulk purchases, sales promotions, and fund-raising, contact Tamara Ellison & Company, LLC Sales at **info@tamaraellison.com**

Visit author's website at **www.tamaraellison.com**

ISBN-13: 9781539790815

ISBN-10: 1539790819

I would like to thank my loving husband, Winston, and our four children for supporting me and allowing me some time to write, grow, and develop as an author.

I want to thank my godmother and my best friend for their prayers and encouragement along the way.

To my Heavenly Father, thank You for providing the grace for me to start and finish the vision that You gave me.

Table Of Contents

Bandages

\#

Painful moments and devastating experiences in life will cause scrapes and bruises, leaving you wounded. When this occurs, a bandage is applied to protect the wounded area. However, if a bandage is left on too long it can cause damage to the skin and become difficult to remove. Thus, the bandage is doing more damage than good and must be removed.

God wants to mend the wound, but He must first peel through the layers of bandages that have been acquired over the years. Some bandages were put on voluntarily as a defense, while others are dirt and debris built up from years of trials, tribulations, and despair. Regardless of how the layer of bandages formed, God is peeling each one away and applying healing to where you hurt.

Day 1

—

Look What They've Done To Me!

Surviving hurt is not easy. In fact, without God it is impossible to be truly made whole. Often you may feel like the person who offended you is prospering. Your husband cheated on you and now they're getting married; you're convinced that they will live happily ever after. Or perhaps your childhood friend betrays you, leaving you broken. It doesn't appear to have affected them at all. They move on quickly to the next friendship without regret. Through the eyes of the victim, the offender's life doesn't seem to be affected in a negative way at all. Everything in you is screaming, "IT'S NOT FAIR! Look what they've done to me!"

My dear Beloved - your Savior, Jesus Christ cares! He is concerned about everything you've had to endure. According to Matthew 10:30, He even keeps a count of the hairs on your head. No matter how big or small the issue, He wants to be involved and become the solution. To begin the mending process, you must believe that He cares and that His promises are true.

Our Focus Passage

Psalms 37:1-4 (NIV)
Do not fret because of evil men or be envious of those who do wrong; for like the grass they will soon wither, like green plants they will soon die away. Trust in the LORD and do good; dwell in the land and enjoy safe pasture. Delight yourself in the LORD, and He will give you the desires of your heart.

God's first request is for you not to fret. Why? Because God is in control and all things are working together for your good. You can't see it now, but when the dust settles from the storm, God's plan will become crystal clear. Yes, growing up without a father was tough, and that divorce almost killed you. However, It gave you the strength and motivation you needed to overcome other difficult issues you encountered in life. When we can't trust God's method, we must trust His heart.

There was a blind man in the Bible who wanted Jesus to heal him. However, Jesus chose the most unorthodox method to perform this miracle. He spat in the dirt and swished it around to make mud cakes, which He then placed over the blind man's eyes. How would placing mud cakes over my eyes help me see? I am sure the blind man had thought this. To make matters more complicated, Jesus then told the blind man to go and wash in the pool. Not only is the man blind, but he now has mud cakes over his eyes. How then does Jesus expect him to find the pool and then wash? When you asked God to heal your heart, it wouldn't make sense for Him to answer your request by telling you to forgive the person that caused you years of pain. Instead of seeking payback or revenge, He commands you to love them and pray for them. Luke 6:28 (NIV) states it best: "bless those who curse you, pray for those who mistreat you." Their action caused your blindness, but trusting in God is your mud cake moment. No, it will not make sense until you wash all the dirt and spit out of your eyes - then you will see how God has healed you.

Why soothe the hurt or cover it when God can heal the pain? All the medicine in the world would not have the power to cure the wounds of your soul. It will just make the pain go away temporarily. To start the healing process, you must give the offender and the pain over to Jesus and obey His word and do "good!" The Scripture continues (Ps 37:3): "dwell in the land and enjoy safe pasture." According to Strong's Concordance, to dwell means: to reside, to inhabit, lay, to remain, or rest. This means that Jesus wants you to live in Him and rest on the fact that He is faithful! Although He did not choose to use your method to deliver you, trust His heart. Christ died for you; why would Jesus abandon you now? God has never failed you, and He is in it for the long haul. Yes, you have scars; but those scars have shaped you into a beautiful vessel that God will use and set out for display for the world to see.

Reflections:

- Trust and do good; trust God even when it seems unfair. Trust God when it seems impossible; trust God! Do good and don't seek revenge or payback. Instead, get involved with positive actions such as singing praises during this valley experience, serving the Lord and His people at your local church, and praying for your enemies. Doing these things will accelerate the mending process in your life. The healing waters will begin to flood the dry and hardened places of the heart.

Stop and think about it.

Prayer

Let's pray: Dear Savior, there is nothing too hard for You. I place my heart in Your hands to do as You please. I release my offenders and enemies, and I forgive them. I want to trust and do good but I need Your help to do it. I seek Your face and desire more of Your spirit. Thank You Lord for not forsaking me and for making me whole. Amen.

Jot down thoughts in your *Capture the Moment Journal.*

Day 2

—

Am I Damaged Goods?

Going through hurt, disappointment, betrayal, and loss will have you wondering if something is wrong with you. You might have thought, *"If I had done this or that, maybe they would still be here."* Maybe if I were prettier, better in bed, skinner, smarter, or shorter, that would not have happened. It's all my fault; **I'm damaged goods!** Because something is damaged most would refuse to pay full price and the damage diminishes the item's value. Now that you feel you are damaged, you've lowered your expectations and discounted your value.

My dear beloved, the Bible is clear; God›s ways are not our ways and His thoughts are not our thoughts (Isaiah 55:8). Hallelujah! Others (and perhaps even you) might view yourself as damaged goods with no purpose. However, you were bought with a high price by the blood of Jesus, who is the precious Lamb of God & the ultimate sacrifice for sin. Just when you felt worthless and invaluable, because of the blood of Jesus you are priceless. In fact, Jeremiah 29:11 says, *"For I know the thoughts that I think towards you, saith the Lord, thoughts of peace, and not of evil, to give you an expected end."* The Lord doesn't see you the way you and others do. He sees you as a woman full of purpose, destiny, and potential. He knows your true worth and paid full price for you because you are worth it.

Our Focus Passage:

Jeremiah 30:17
For I will restore health to you and heal you of your wounds says the Lord because they called you an outcast. Saying this is Zion no one seeks her.

Let's talk about it.

God wants to heal your thoughts. Heal my thoughts, you ask? Yes, I know you think you suffer from a broken heart, but it's not your heart that was offended; it was your mind. Jesus died so that you can be free of guilt, torment, hurt, anger, abandonment, mistreatment, and abuse.

Question: Do you believe the thoughts of God about you and your life?

"For I will restore" is how our focus passage begins. To restore something, according to the Webster Dictionary, is to give back someone or something that was lost or taken. As you look over your life and see the things that were taken or lost, God has promised to restore them!!! He is not a man that He should lie (Numbers 23:19), so if He said it, it will come to pass. However, because of what was lost or taken, it may be difficult to believe and trust in God. Yet, God›s faithfulness to His promise is not predicated on you believing! Jesus still loves you beyond your fears.

Does this mean that He will allow you to remain in a 'woe is me, I›m the victim' state? Absolutely not. John 10:10 tells us, "He came that we might have LIFE!" So it›s time to start living a healthy life, mentally and physically. God said that He will restore you. He is healing those wounds; even the ones that you tried to mend but it left an ugly scar on your life. How, you might ask? By looking at the scars, wounds, and cuts as a qualifier instead of a disqualifier. Our focus passage states that God will restore and heal because you were an outcast!!! He came to restore your life not to the state before the pain occurred, but to restore it to the state that is covered in the precious blood of Jesus Christ, as a new creature.

Reflections:

- Because you were considered an outcast or damaged goods, this made you a candidate for God to move and heal all your sorrows, and pains.
- God knows your insecurities and will help you overcome them by tearing down the lies you have heard and believed over the years.
- The Lord will build you up with expressing His thoughts of love and plans to prosper you.

Stop and think about it.

Prayer

Let's pray: Dear Jehovah Rapha, our Healer, there is nothing too hard for you. I place my heart in your hands to do as you please. I release my offenders and enemies, and I forgive them. Restore me and heal the wounds in my mind, for your name's sake. I confess your thoughts towards me oh God, and will no longer walk in agreement with any other confession that does not agree with your thoughts. I declare my wounds have been healed and I no longer carry the shameful scars because I have been restored in Jesus name! Amen.

Jot down thoughts in your *Capture the Moment Journal.*

Day 3

—

Let It Go!

TThere are times when you want to go back into the abusive relationship and/or the habit that God has delivered you from, but you must hold fast. You will even go overboard, trying to be a super Christian and attempt to deliver yourself by works. Fellowship is key, but you can sleep under the pews at church, and that in itself has no saving power. Galatians 5:2 states, "Indeed I, Paul say to you that if you become circumcised, Christ will profit you nothing." To be circumcised is to cut the extra foreskin or flesh, and although you have cut off things, people and habits, you still cannot move past the torment in your mind. Rejecting Jesus because you feel unworthy is the crutch you lean on instead of the Rock, Jesus Christ. Going through the rituals and church edicts cannot deliver nor keep you. Only the grace and mercy of our Lord and Savior can do that, and He never runs out. The grace and mercy account is replenished every morning. (Yes God!!)

Dear beloved you can cast all of your cares on the Lord. He is waiting on you to let it go. In order to do so, you have to trust God with every fiber of your being. The word of the Lord says in Proverbs 3:5 (KJV) "Trust in the Lord with all your heart, and lean not unto thine own understanding." You have had to protect, defend, and provide for yourself for so long that you think that you have a good understanding on how to take care of you. However, God's ways are not limited to your understanding. Who would want to serve a God that they could outthink?

Our Focus Passage:

Galatians 5:1(NKJV)
Stand fast therefore in the liberty by which Christ has made us free, and do not be entangled again with a yoke of bondage.

Let's talk about it.

"Stand fast" is to be firmly fixed into a place or position regardless of the obstacles, temptation, doubts, and fears (**www.merriam-webster.com**). You must hold on to God's promise of mending your broken mind, and making you new. Yes, winds are going to blow and everyday will not feel like a win, but you must "Stand Fast."

Question: What are some things, thoughts, and/or people causing you to hold on to the past and walk away from your future?

Everything we need was completed at Calvary. The Bible informs us that Christ died before the foundation of the world (Revelation 13:8), so before you even existed to have a problem, God provided the answer. However, we tend to lean to our own understanding and rely on past experiences to guide our judgment. Life can be a bully, and what you had to endure seems unfair, and undeserved; however, we are commanded to stand fast. Abraham and Sarah were given a promise and they attempted to help God out. Their own understanding told them they were too old to have children. Instead of standing fast, they doubted and relied on what they thought was best. However, God was not intimidated by their doubts, and once they were determined to trust God with all their heart, Isaac, the promise, was born. Although Abraham was not perfect and he doubted God sometimes, he was still considered a man of faith by God. The blood of Jesus Christ covers all sins, and although we are not perfect, we can come boldly before the throne of grace and release our cares, torments, pains, shortcomings and emotions to our Heavenly Father. We cannot understand everything, but we just need to remember that Christ has made us free. Although we do not deserve His love, we don't need to feel unworthy. Jesus loved us and decided to die for an imperfect you and me. Galatians 5:1 also tells us not to be entangled with bondage anymore. You are no longer a slave to your emotions and life experiences. You can let go of self-pity, disappointment, hatred, anger, fear, and loneliness in the face and scream, "I am FREE!"

Reflections:

- Hold on to the promise of a restored and mended heart and never let go.
- Stand fast and don't go back to the yoke of bondage. You have been set FREE.
- Although you're not perfect, it is Christ's blood that redeems you. Self-pity, low self-esteem, anger, depression, and hatred can no longer hold you captive.

Stop and think about it.

Prayer:

Let's pray: Dear Father, my Protector, there is nothing too hard for you. I place my heart in your hands to do as you please. I release my offenders and enemies, and I forgive them. I let go of the emotions holding me back from seeing You in every area of my life. I let go, and give control of my life, and I yield to the Holy Spirit. I will stand fast and wait on the promises of God. I believe I am healed from every emotional scar and I am no longer a slave to my past and to my emotion; I am Free. I declare I have Joy, Peace, and Love in my life and in my heart my wounds have been healed. In the name that is above everything, Jesus Christ! Amen.

Jot down thoughts in your *Capture the Moment Journal.*

Day 4

—

Some Days I Just Don't Feel Like It!

Sometimes, life can seem like one huge challenge that you don't feel like overcoming today. You don't want to pursue anything; you just want to be left alone.

"I just don't feel like it!" you might say.

These are signs of depression, and out of all the layers, it's very thick and grows over the heart. Depression is a weed in a very beautiful garden. Although everything is blooming around you, the focus becomes the weed, and it begins to suck the life out of the other flowers. However, there is help; God wants to do an exchange with you. He wants to trade beauty for your ashes, a garment of praise in exchange for your garment of heaviness. *Psalms 30:11 (NKJV): "You have turned my mourning into dancing; You have put off my sackcloth and clothed me with gladness."* Praise God! For this will be your testimony and the world will know it.

Dear Beloved, there is no pit too dark or too deep that Jesus cannot reach in and save you. This is not a fairy tale; this is real. He is your Hero, Superman, Avenger, Knight in shining armor, and Your Prince of Peace. He is not afraid to come into your dark and lonely world and carry you out! David reminds us in Psalms 139:7-8 (NIV) *"Where can I go from your Spirit? Where can I flee from your presence? If I go up to the heavens, you are there; If I make my bed in the depths, you are there."* Jesus is wherever you're reading this: in the bed, in the kitchen, at work, or in the tub - He can meet you right where you are.

Our Focus Passage

Isaiah 61:3 (NKJV)

To console those who mourn in Zion, to give them beauty for ashes, the oil of joy for mourning, the garment of praise for the spirit of heaviness; That they may be called trees of righteousness, the planting of the Lord, that He may be glorified.

Let's talk about it.

God loves you and He's here to console you! He doesn't care about your past, because He knew about it when it was still considered your future. He wants to do a trade with you. Now most people will trade things that have a similar value; however, the trade that God wants to perform in your life is not worth to be compared to the Glory that will be revealed (Romans 8:18). He wants your ashes.

During Biblical times, ashes were used as a sign of great grief. God wants your pain. The pain or grief could have been caused by great loss or death. Perhaps the death of a loved one has occurred, or the relationship that you thought would last forever has ended. You may have chosen not to go through with the pregnancy, and even suicidal thoughts can be tormenting your mind. However, God says, *"I will take your ashes, your grief, and your sorrows in exchange for my beauty."* This is not an equal value trade, but God is willing to pay more than what you might think you're worth, simply because He loves you. You can't change His mind about you. He paid the ultimate price, which was the blood of His beloved son Jesus. In Biblical times they would cover themselves with ashes and tear their garments. Could you imagine the visual? They wanted to demonstrate outwardly how they felt on the inside; they felt torn, dirty, and hopeless. That is why God's trade starts with beauty. He will reach down past the grief and pain and give you hope, joy, peace, and a promise.

The oil of joy for mourning is the next trade. Oil was used for a variety of reasons during Biblical times, but one of the main purposes was to anoint. David went from shepherd boy to king once he was anointed. Aaron was just Moses' brother until he was anointed; then he became a priest. God is transforming you, Hallelujah! He is anointing you with the oil of joy. You once were depressed, in pain, grieving and hopeless, and you felt like giving up on everything, but now you are full of his joy. Nehemiah 8:10 says *"For this day is holy unto our Lord: neither be ye sorry; the joy of the Lord is our strength"*. No more regrets, no more self-pity, no more woe is me, or I can't do this or that, no more complaints." Just as

Jesus told the paralyzed man in John 5:8 *"Rise, take up your bed and walk,"* He has declared in your life walk, to dust yourself off and take the beauty and joy, and live again.

The next trade is a garment of praise for a spirit of heaviness. Notice that the heaviness is a spirit, and not something natural. We are no match for spiritual warfare without Christ, so instead of leaving you to contend with a spirit of heaviness, He gives you a garment of praise. That garment of praise is a choice; you can choose to wear it. I often think of Superman, as when he was Clark Kent he was considered weak, shy, and a pushover. However, when needed, he would change into his Superman cape and save the day. Well, God has given you your own cape! While you are consumed with heaviness, you're weak, defeated, hopeless, and depressed. Yet when you put on your garment of praise, you are declaring that you are victorious, a champion, strong, more than a conqueror, and at perfect peace.

Reflections:
- God wants to make a trade with you; He will take your pain, hurt, and grief in exchange for joy, peace, and victory.
- Never give up hope; never quit, and don't doubt. God is delivering you. Declare and stand on Romans 8:31, that God is for you. He is on your side, so you will win.

Stop and think about it.

Prayer:
Let's pray: Oh God, the lifter of my head, I release the spirit of heaviness to You now. Give me the garment of praise. Deliver me from the pain of my past. I want to trade all the hurt, grief and disappointment in exchange for Your victory, peace and joy. I can't do this alone. I have tried and failed, but with You I am more than a conqueror. I am victorious in you and the spirit of heaviness has no place in my life! I am no longer ruled by depression. I am free, and free indeed. I declare that I have joy, peace, and love in my life and in my heart, and my wounds have been healed. In the name that is above everything, Jesus Christ! Amen.

Jot down thoughts in your *Capture the Moment Journal.*

Day 5

—

I Hate You!

Based on what has happened to you; most might say you have the right to be angry. You even agree that you are justified in harboring anger. Maybe your innocence was stolen, or someone ruined your life and left you in pieces. You may hate them, and never want to forgive them. You may want revenge for what was done to you. You want justice! You may want the other person to pay and feel the same hurt that you are now forced to live with. This, my beloved, is Anger; and this layer will destroy you if not released. The Lord has not turned a blind eye to what happened to you. Roman 12:19 (NIV) states, "Do not take revenge, my dear friends, but leave room for God's wrath, for it is written: ""It is mine to avenge; I will repay," says the Lord."

Now if God says He will repay, He will, but it is not our job to ask where, when and how. Although you feel angry, mad and frustrated, our hope is in Jesus - not in the "repay." There is comfort in knowing that the God of everything is protective of His precious creation and He cares. Being a good Father, He will fight for you, but His main concern is you, not your enemies. God wants you whole, free, and mended. You must not allow anger to govern your life. You must forgive and let go of your troubles. 1 Peter 5:7 states, "casting all your anxiety on Him, because He cares for you." God cares, but they did not care about what would happen to you. They took what they wanted, and did what they wanted regardless of how it would affect you. However, that is not the end of your story; the next chapters of your life are greater. Romans 8:18 sums it up best: "For I reckon that the sufferings of this present time are not worthy to be compared with the glory which shall be revealed in us (KJV)."

Our Focus Passage

Ephesians 4:26-27 (NIV)

And "don't sin by letting anger control you." Don't let the sun go down while you are still angry, 27 for anger gives a foothold to the devil.

Let's talk about it.

Notice that anger itself is not the sin, but letting it control you is. God does not expect for you to live life without emotion, but we are accountable for them. If you are angry with someone, you should handle it immediately. Often times, it includes praying for that person or situation right then and there, and releasing it into the Lord's hands.

Luke 6:28 (KJV): "Bless them that curse you, and pray for them which despitefully use you."

At times even the Lord Himself was angry (Deuteronomy 9:8), but He did not let it control Him. Anger can stop you from loving again or trusting again. You may be tempted to believe that you can control anger, but you can't. Anger can cause you to become bitter, mad, and frustrated with everyone and everything. Years have passed and you have not confronted and released the anger. Sure, you are great at masking it and pretending to be okay, but you are raging inside. You may be self-abusive or you're entering relationships with the same cycle of abuse, disappointment and rejection. Most will try to fight their emotion and trouble as if it is that easy. Ephesians 6:12 informs us that this is a spiritual battle.

The spiritual battle can only be won by using spiritual weapons. One of the most powerful weapons is forgiveness. Beloved, you must forgive! The only one who suffers is you. Most of the people you are angry with are nowhere to be found, dead, or they've moved on. However, you are the one who is trapped and locked up by anger. However, God wants to remove the bandage of Anger and set you free. No pain, grief, or sorrow can withstand the blood of Jesus. Give it to Him and His blood will wash away the anger, and make you whole again.

John 8:36 (KJV): "If the Son therefore shall make you free, ye shall be free indeed."

Reflections:

- It is okay to feel the emotion of anger. However, it is not okay to let it build up and linger without giving it to the Lord.
- Forgive the person or situation that offended you and pray for your enemies.
- No matter how deep-rooted the anger may be, nothing is greater than the healing and saving power of our Lord and Savior Jesus Christ.

Stop and think about it.

Prayer:

Let's pray: My Savior and King, I release the spirit of anger to You now. I pray for that person who hurt me; save and deliver them. I give them to You, Lord. Let Your will be done in their lives. I also pray for their families, and for their lives. Allow them to have an encounter with You, Lord, and cleanse them from all of their shortcomings. I unlock the door to my heart, so please come in. I've tried to protect myself and pretend to be okay, but I am not. Save me from the anger due to my experiences and encounters. I believe that whom the Son has set free, is free indeed (John 8:36). Give me the strength to deal with my emotion quickly and give it to You. I am victorious in You, and the spirit of anger has no place in my life! I am no longer ruled by hatred and frustration. I am free, and free indeed. I believe that I am healed from every emotional scar and I am no longer a slave to my past and emotion. I am free. I declare that I have joy, peace, and love in my life and heart. My wounds have been healed and mended. Amen.

Jot down thoughts in your *Capture the Moment Journal.*

Day 6

—

I'm Fine; I Don't Need Your Help!

It's a rare trait in today's society to find someone who is dependable. It is the norm for a person to say whatever they want in order to get what they want, and often they go back on their word. Depending on an unreliable person can be very frustrating. This is often seen in relationships, where commitments are made and eventually broken. A couple gets married, and declares in front of witnesses, "until death do us part." However, when the slightest bump occurs, they want a divorce. A business partner makes plans to take on a big investment, but backs out and leaves you with the expenses.

When you have had disappointment after disappointment, you give up on trusting people, and sometimes on God. Their promises seem empty and void, and although you want to trust them, you can't. To avoid further disappointment, you develop a defense mechanism of independence. Everything could be going wrong in your life, but when offered help you respond, "I'm fine, I don't need your help!" Even when God tries to step in, you will refuse His provisions.

Beloved, God's help is a well that never runs dry. God does not force you to take His help; you must first admit, "I need help!"

Our Focus Passage
Matthew 8:23-26 (NIV)
Then he got into the boat and his disciples followed him. Suddenly a furious storm came up on the lake, so that the waves swept over the boat. But Jesus was sleeping. The disciples went and woke him, saying, "Lord, save us! We're going to drown!" He replied, "You of little faith, why are you so afraid?" Then he got up and rebuked the winds and the waves, and it was completely calm.

God will allow circumstances to put you in a place that you can't control. Jesus had worked many miracles at this point in his ministry. After being with Jesus, the disciples should have known that He was going to take care of them. Yet, they relied on their knowledge, as most of them were fishermen and knew how to navigate the sea. I could imagine them trying all of the techniques and methods that they knew to navigate the boat through that storm. It was at that moment they realized that they needed help. We need someone who is far greater than our strength and capability.

You have tried to work out every possible angle in your situation, but nothing is working. Some would rather fail than to have to admit they need help, or that they need to depend on anyone. The thought of trusting again releases a paralyzing fear that keeps you from trusting in your Heavenly Father. You may be filtering everything through a heart that has been clogged with the dirt of disappointment, rejection, abandonment and pain. For example, an air filter's main function is to keep out harmful particles from the air, and only allow the clean air to pass through. However, if the filter is dirty or clogged, it will allow the dirt and particles to pass through or in some cases, it will restrict the proper airflow and cause major damage. We must ask God to clean the filter of our hearts and minds so that we can filter out the doubt, lack of trust, disappointment and unforgiveness, and allow the clean air to flow through. Remember that man's promises can fail and you may experience disappointment; however, God is not a man that He is capable of lying, nor will one of His words fall to the ground.

No matter how many promises God has made, they are "Yes" in Christ.
"And so through him the "Amen" that is spoken by us is unto the glory of God."
2 Corinthians 1:20 (NIV)

Reflections:

- Although we have experienced disappointment, God is not to be placed in this category. For His word is true, and if He said it, He will perform it.
- Being independent is not a bad thing; however, God desires that we trust and rely on Him. Our Heavenly Father is waiting to remove the burdens that we should never bear.
- Although you may have rejected His love and provision at one point, He awaits the day for you to invite Him into your life again so that He may show Himself strong.

Stop and think about it.

Prayer:

Let's pray: Oh Father, I need you. I have tried to do life on my own, and it is not working. I admit that I need Your help. I forgive those who have disappointed me and I forgive myself for trusting the wrong people. I am nothing without you God; You are my hope, my help, my plan, my answer, and my life. Wash the filter of my heart and mind, and remove the debris of disappointment so that I can attract the things that You intend for me, Lord.

I acknowledge that You are the source of my strength, and despite my actions You have never left me nor forsaken me. Please take my burdens that I have tried to prove that I can carry on my own. You are a present help in the time of trouble; help me to see that (Psalms 46:1). God, sometimes life seems unfair, but I will call upon You and I know that You will answer. I release my control and I'll allow You to lead the way. Guide every step and mend the areas of disappointment. Thank You God for Your faithfulness towards me during my unfaithfulness to You. In Jesus name I pray, Amen.

Jot down thoughts in your ***Capture the Moment*** Journal.

Day 7

—

Did God Forget About Me?

As we go through life, there are times where we might feel as if God has forgotten about us. Surely He has more important things to do, such as balancing the universe and holding the stars in place. We imagine that our prayer requests are submitted through God's prayer hotline, and we are on hold, in queue, ready to be answered in the order received. The delay leaves you asking yourself, "Did God Forget About Me?" A mother's love is used to describe the most faithful and pure love, but even a mother's love can't compare to God's love for you! Matthew 7:11 explains it best: "If you, then, though you are evil, know how to give good gifts to your children, how much more will your Father in heaven give good gifts to those who ask him!" When someone is forgotten, it communicates to them that they were not a priority or as important. However, if you were the only one on earth, Jesus would have died and endured the rejection, torture, and death just for you!

Beloved, God knows your cry and plea, and out of the billions of people in the world, your voice is unique and has a special place in His heart. According to Isaiah 49:16 (NLT), He knows you by name. God has written your name on the palm of His hand, so you can never be forgotten!

Our Focus Passage

Isaiah 49:15 NIV
"Can a mother forget the baby at her breast and have no compassion on the child she has borne? Though she may forget, I will not forget you!"

Let's talk about it.

We forget lots of things, like stopping at the grocery store, or paying a bill by a certain date. However, there are certain things we don't forget, such as going to work or taking the kids to school. They are second nature and a part of our life. However, we have all experienced that time when someone you were depending on to be there forgot to show up. The thought of someone not caring enough about you or something that was important to you hurts! Although they may apologize, the excuse "I forgot" doesn't suffice, and trust is lost! Who doesn't want to be important or on the list of priorities? This is how we feel when we pray and it seems like God is so far away. Did He not hear me? Is God too busy to check on little ole me? To make matters worse, days, weeks, months and years pass as you wait for your request to be fulfilled. We think that just because we followed the '5 Steps To Getting Our Prayers Answered Guide' that it will provoke God into action. God gave His Son Jesus before you had a problem, because He is provoked by His own love for you to come to your aid and send you a Savior. We take God's delay as a denial or oversight, but there are no mistakes in God.

God's response to your question, "Did God forget about me?" is answered in Isaiah 49:15 "Can a mother forget..." though she may, I cannot. God uses the love and a bond of a mother to her nursing infant to prove His love. Anyone who has nursed or fed a child knows you can't forget him or her. Yet, God says if for some strange reason you did forget about your child, I could never forget about you! God takes the time to number the hairs on your head (Luke 27:12) and cause his mercy to follow you and He replenishes His mercy each morning (Lam. 3:22). Every time God looks at his hand, He sees you, for Isaiah 49:16 (NLT) states: "See, I have engraved you on the palms of my hands; your walls are ever before me." Not only does He have you tattooed on the palm of His hand, "your walls are ever before me" or in other words, the thing, problem, circumstance, or challenge that has walled you in: God sees it. He sees and will make a way of escape for you every time.

Reflections:

- God's delay is not a denial, and although his provision is prolonged, He will rescue, deliver, heal, restore, and provide.
- God is provoked by His own love toward us, to provide a way of escape from our troubles. And even if we have fallen short, His grace and mercy are new every morning, and they are ready to cover us throughout our day.
- People may forget, but God cannot forget. His love for you won't let Him. He sees the walls in your life and is concerned about every detail in your life.

Prayer

Let's pray: My Lord and Savior, thank you for remembering me in my time of trouble. I will cry out to You oh Lord, and You will save me from my shame, and disappointment. Dear Lord, when trouble arises, cause me to remember Your faithfulness and to trust Your Word to light up the dark places in my life. I trust You when I cannot feel You, and I trust You when I cannot see You. Jesus, thank you for reminding me that Your love won't let you forget about me. I am special and precious in your sight, despite my mistakes. Thank You for never forgetting about me! Amen.

Jot down thoughts in your *Capture the Moment Journal.*

Day 8

—

I Give Up; Nothing Is Going To Change!

Have you ever experienced a trial that you thought would last longer than you could bear? We start off with the hope that everything will work out for good. Yet, after months and years go by, the flame of hope starts to dwindle. Eventually the flame goes out and hope is lost. You have prayed for financial breakthrough, healing in your body, restoration of a marriage, salvation of a loved one, or deliverance in your emotions and you still haven't received the breakthrough that you so desperately longed for. Although you appear to be strong, you have just learned how to function with the pain and ignore your feelings of hopelessness. You're going through the motions and accepting what life has dealt you. With your mouth you pretend to be encouraged, saying things like, "I am trusting God," but in your heart you're screaming, "God, I give up! Nothing is going to change!"

However, Beloved, you don't have to pretend with God, for He knows your heart. I am reminded of the passage in Mark 9:14-24 when a man brought his son to Jesus to be healed from evil spirits. The boy's father explained that he tried to believe. He had even brought his son to the disciples and they could not cast the evil spirit out (Mark 9:18). Perhaps you feel this way about your situation. You submitted the prayer request, sought counsel from spiritual leaders, and attended the conference, but still no change. However, the father in the story says something that I believe released his breakthrough and gave him victory. In Mark 9:24 the father said to Jesus, "I do believe, but help me overcome my unbelief!" He was honest!! Yes, you believe that Jesus can do anything, yet in certain circumstances you need God to help your unbelief. He will not only restore your hope, but He will rebuke the evil spirits that have plagued you and they will never return. Hallelujah!

Our Focus Passage

1 Samuel 1:19-20 (NLT)
The entire family got up early the next morning and went to worship the LORD once more. Then they returned home to Ramah. When Elkanah slept with Hannah, the LORD remembered her plea, and in due time she gave birth to a son. She named him Samuel for she said, "I asked the LORD for him."

Let's talk about it.

Many of us are familiar with the story of Hannah, but let's look further into her life story. This was a woman who believed God for a child. Hannah had prayed, worshiped, and attended church year after year only to go home with a barren womb. Hannah's husband, Elkanah, had another wife named Peninnah who was an evil woman. 1 Samuel 1:6 explained how Peninnah would taunt Hannah and make fun of her because she was not able to have children. It wasn't enough for Hannah to bear the shame of being cursed (in biblical times, women were believed to be cursed by God if they were barren), but she had to endure Peninnah's baby showers, 1st birthday parties, and play-dates with other moms. I could imagine her wanting to give up. The Bible tells us that she prayed and did all that was required of her, yet her breakthrough had not come.

In life we are faced with situations that we cannot control, and we've attempted to do all that we know is right to do. However, it still feels as if there is no hope. Years and years are passing by without any signs of the situation changing. Just like Hannah, you pray and worship God and are living a righteous lifestyle, but yet it seems like those who live a God-free life are experiencing the joy, hope, and blessing that you've have been praying for. This story might hit close to home for those who are believing God for a child, but whatever you are believing God for, just know that hope is not lost.

I love Hannah's determination in 1 Samuel 1:8-11. She starts off crying and feeling sorry for herself. She is so down that even her husband's encouraging words aren't helping. However, the turning point comes at verse 9 where "Hannah got up and went to pray." She left her pity party and rose above the valley of despair and called on God one more time.

I challenge you to get up for your valley of despair and call on your Savior, Jesus Christ, one more time. Although hope was gone, Hannah asked God to help her unbelief to help her get past what she saw and heard, and cause her to believe. Although hope seems lost, this is what you must do. Romans 4:18 (NLT) describes it best: "Against all hope, Abraham in hope believed and so became the father of many nations..."

Reflections:
- All hope is not lost, but you must hope against the odds and endure until your change comes.
- Rise above your valley of despair and frustration and follow Hannah's example; pray and believe.

Prayer

Let's pray: Dear Lord of my breakthrough, I thank You that when my peace fled, You became my peace. When all hope was lost, You found me and became my hope. My life is in Your hands and I find safety in Your arms. Hide me in your presence that I may block out all the negativity going on around me, and I can see Your grace and power that surrounds me. I trust You Lord; however, help my unbelief. When the enemy comes in like a flood, I thank You for lifting up a standard to protect my loved ones and me. When I can't see Your hand of provision, teach me how to trust Your heart and the love that You have for me. Amen.

Jot down thoughts in your *Capture the Moment Journal.*

Day 9

—

What Was I Thinking?

We endure ups and downs, as it is a natural course of life. However, when those trials are a result of poor decisions, the trial may end, but the feelings of regret remain. The issue was over 10 years ago and life has moved on, but we can't help but fall prey to harsh self-criticism and regret. Reflecting on a life before the situation occurred will have us mentally painting a picture of bliss and tranquility. "What was I thinking? If I only had left sooner or said no in the beginning!" We make decisions in haste in order to get what we want NOW. Later we discover what we wanted and the method used to get it caused more harm than good.

However, Beloved, God was not intimidated by our clouded judgment, nor was He caught off guard. God knew we would decide to go without consulting Him, ignore his warnings, or deliberately defy Him to get what we wanted, but His grace is sufficient. God has a way of taking a mistake and turning it into something beautiful for His glory. Beloved, He takes the worst part of our stories and causes us to rise in victory. Forgive yourself and know that all things, not just the nice and pleasant things, but also the dark and painful things, will work out for your good.

Our Focus Passage
2 Corinthians 4:17-18 (NLT)
For our present troubles are small and won't last very long. Yet they produce for us a glory that vastly outweighs them and will last forever! 18 So we don't look at the troubles we can see now; rather, we fix our gaze on things that cannot be seen. For the things we see now will soon be gone, but the things we cannot see will last forever.

Let's talk about it.

If you had an opportunity to go back in time, what would you change? Perhaps you would have chosen a different career, focused more in school, or married more carefully. However, God is the Author and Finisher of our faith (Hebrews 12:2). In other words, He is the Author of your book entitled Life. What makes a great story is not just the happily ever after, but the suspense, drama, and betrayal in between. Not one single chapter in your life could be extracted from your book as each trial and triumph is uniquely joined together. The death of the loved one made you stronger, the disappointment birthed resilience, and the tragedy equipped you with endurance.

What you've experienced in your life was designed to destroy you, but the enemy (Satan) did not realize that it would allow God to get the glory out of your life. Consider our focus passage; the present troubles, emotional withdrawal, and mental fatigue will last just for a little while. Why does God consider our troubles "small" when to us they feel like mighty mountains? Simple, because the glory they produce is larger, deeper, greater, and wider than any trouble you can experience. God is trying to put everything into the right perspective so that we can realize that He will use everything we regret, to shape our destiny. We see our issues as mountains, and yet He says our faith is larger than the mountains we face. Jesus explains in Mark 11:23 (NIV), "Truly I tell you, if anyone says to this mountain, 'Go, throw yourself into the sea,' and does not doubt in their heart but believes that what they say will happen, it will be done for them."

Yes, the trial drained you emotionally, but we are not to focus on the situation, which are the things we can see. We are to focus on what we can't see with our natural eyes but is clear as day in the spirit. 2 Corinthians 4:18 states, "So we don't look at the troubles we can see now; rather, we fix our gaze on things that cannot be seen. For the things we see now will soon be gone, but the things we cannot see will last forever." God's promises that He will restore and we will recover what was lost. Yet, the picture is invisible and nearly impossible to see as it is covered with layers of regret and disappointments. Now is the time to let it go! The truth is you are not a victim, bitter, or angry but you are FORGIVEN and by grace you will rise above troubles and come out victorious!

Stop and think about it.

Prayer

Let's pray: Our God, Savior, and Friend, You see our flaws and continue to love us all the more. Despite our insecurities and shortcomings there is one thing we are confident in, that You desire for us to dwell in Your presence. In Your presence is where we'll find peace and the encouragement we need. We thank You for loving us past our silly reasoning, thinking that we can do it on our own. But today we no longer focus on the mistakes of our past but we focus on the things that the natural eye can't see. We see the change; we are coming out of our cave of despair into the brightness of your love. Thank You for teaching me how to let go when I want to hold on. Thank you Jesus! Amen.

Jot down thoughts in your *Capture the Moment Journal.*

Day 10

—

I Want To Just Go and Hide!

We can appreciate transparency to certain degree, but there some things we can't tell anyone. The shame we experienced causes us to **want to just go and hide** in an attempt to escape shame and ridicule. Often the shame is the result of an unsolicited event, abuse, molestation, rape, public rejection, and disappointment. It is the lack of acceptance or having your innocence taken that brings about shame. A failed attempt at trying to maintain a false image leads one to avoid facing the truth, to avoid shame. Once the feeling of shame comes, the human instinct is to run and hide to cover the wounds and escape the humiliation. Yet, not all is lost, for we find hope in God's Word.

Beloved, He takes the ugly, embarrassing things in life and covers them with His blood. Although you want to run and hide in depression, alcohol, cigarettes, sex, gambling, or overspending, God gives us a hiding place where we can be made whole and be restored. Psalms 27:5 (NIV) states "For in the day of trouble he will keep me safe in his dwelling; he will hide me in the shelter of his sacred tent and set me high upon a rock." I love this verse because while the goal of "shame" is to makes you feel low; but God lifts you up from your low state and sets you HIGH upon a rock.

Our Focus Passage

Isaiah 54:4 (NIV)
"Do not be afraid; you will not be put to shame. Do not fear disgrace; you will not be humiliated. You will forget the shame of your youth and remember no more the reproach of your widowhood."

Let's talk about it.

The first thing God says is "Do not be afraid," which is the first step to overcoming. However, in order to not be afraid, you must have confidence or reassurance in something. 1 John 3:21 helps us understand what we are to be confident in: "And this is the confidence that we have before Him: If we ask anything according to His will, He hears us." The key to seeing total deliverance is in knowing that God hears, sees, and He will respond to your cry. He can be trusted with the secret things. There is a story in the Bible, found in the book of Luke chapter 15 about the prodigal son. The Bible records that the son wanted his inheritance from his father before time, however it did not go well. The prodigal son had made a foolish decision in leaving his father's house by demanding his inheritance. However, despite the circumstances, the prodigal son decides to go back home, and was surprised by his father's response to his return. Luke 15:20 records, "But while he was still a long way off, his father saw him and was filled with compassion for him; he ran to his son, threw his arms around him and kissed him." His father did not refuse him and your heavenly Father will not refuse you. Often we run away from God's presence trying to avoid shame, guilt, and, "I told you so," yet our Heavenly Father is waiting for us to come back to Him and allow Him to remove the shame.

This is the reason you should not be afraid; whatever the circumstance, "you will not be put to shame. Do not fear disgrace; you will not be put to shame." (Isaiah 54:4 NIV) God the Father is waiting with open arms to receive you and your issues, while bidding you to come boldly into His presence. The latter part of our focus passage explains that you will not remember the reproach. It's not saying you will not be able to recall the circumstance, but you will no longer be moved by the pain, guilt, and shame. The power of forgiveness is strong enough to heal all wounds, no matter how deep. This is why Christ forgives us and gives us the power to forgive others and ourselves, thus removing the guilt and shame. This allows you to walk in total victory.

Reflections:

- God is your hiding place in the time of trouble or disappointment. You don't have to bury yourself in other things to cope with your problem.
- You can trust God with your secrets, the things you would never tell anyone.

Stop and think about it.

Prayer

Let us pray: Dear Lord, we praise Your name. We thank You for lifting us up out depression and heartache and establishing us in a high place. Lord, You are my rock, the rock of my salvation. You are the Lord of our salvation, saving us from the shame of our past. The things we wish we could forget, You helped me not to remember them. You have restored our joy and peace; thank you. The areas where I am insecure, You are my confidence and my surety. I trust You with the secrets of my heart and know that You will bring deliverance and restore hope. Amen.

Jot down thoughts in your *Capture the Moment Journal.*

The Recovery Experience

↻

Every injury has a recovery period; that is a part of the healing process. Now that the bandages have been removed, God has prescribed you a time to recover to ensure complete healing. However, this recovery period is not one of rest alone, but restoration. During this recovery period, you will recuperate from the damage that the injury caused, and the Lord will restore your joy, peace, love, confidence, and strength. In the natural, while in recovery, you learn how to use the injured part of your body. God is not just going to remove the hurt, but He will teach your heart how to trust and love again. He will strengthen the muscles of hope, joy, and confidence; all while you're learning how to walk by faith again. Eventually you will see yourself as whole and complete without breaks, fractures, or wounds.

Day 11

—

Growing in God's Grace

Experiencing God's grace is a powerful and life-changing encounter. Through His grace, we have access to salvation, and through salvation, we have access to restoration. Grace is not just unmerited favor; it is the essence of God and His redemption power. Because of grace, Jesus died for everyone's sins so that we could access God's presence without restriction. What is grace? It is the power of God to restore, to change, to become, to have, to overcome, to receive, and to forgive (Heb 4:16 NIV) When I think of grace, I am reminded of a video game I played as a child called Pac-Man. Ghost-like enemies would try to keep him from going through the maze. However, when Pac-Man seemed cornered and without hope, all he had to do was eat a power pellet. After eating a power pellet, he would have the ability to pursue and devour the enemy that once chased him.

Beloved, grace is like the power pellet. As we go through the maze of life, we need a power source greater than our own, and the Grace of God is just that. Giving us this innate ability to love when we want to hate, to trust when we want to doubt, to receive when we should be refused.

Our Focus Passage

2 Corinthians 12:9 NIV
But he said to me, "My grace is sufficient for you, for my power is made perfect in weakness." Therefore, I will boast all the more gladly about my weaknesses so that Christ's power may rest on me.

Let's talk about it.

We all encounter hardships and difficulties in the maze called life and instead of seeking out a power pellet we would rather be taken out of the maze altogether. Yet, life comes with uncertainties, rewards, and challenges. This is a reality that cannot be escaped. However, God's grace is sufficient! The weaker you feel or become, the stronger the power of God becomes in your life. That is why we must grow in grace. The first thought when trouble arises is self-preservation. We are not as concerned about offenses as much as we are about defense. Yet, you could never win a game with defense alone. If the primary objective is only to stop the other team from scoring, no one will win the game because no one has scored. Grace is an offensive play and puts you in a position to win. Think about it; , you survived the divorce when it drove others to substance abuse. You survived the housing market crash when others saw no way out other than to give up. You came out of the fiery trails of life smoke-free simply because of the grace of God.

When you watch the famous ballet Swan Lake, you will be captivated by how gracefully the ballerinas perform; it appears to be effortless. You don't get to see the swollen ankles, broken toes, fails and frustration that take place during practice and behind the scenes. People will never truly know your testimony because grace makes it seems effortless. We discussed what grace is, and sometimes we forget that God's power or strength is made perfect in our weakness. This means we can boast in our inability and glorify God's ability. He is your strength, hope, and victory! 2 Corinthians 12:10 (NIV) states, "That is why, for Christ's sake, I delight in weaknesses, in insults, in hardships, in persecutions, in difficulties. For when I am weak, then I am strong."

God is indeed faithful to every word, and now that we have removed the layers that were blocking access to Him, we must now learn to apply grace. The grace that is needed to be a great parent, an honest person, a true friend, a Christian, a faithful spouse, a fair business partner, a champion, a focused student, and everything that life encompasses. He never expected us to do it on our own, but He extended grace so that we could experience life more abundantly. John 10:10 (KJV) states, "The thief, cometh not, but for to steal, and to kill, and to destroy: I am come that they might have life, and that they might have it more abundantly."

Reflections:

- God has given us the power to conquer and overcome every situation. It's called grace.
- Grace must be applied to those areas where personal ability has been exhausted. This is how God's power is made perfect in our weakness.

Stop and think about it.

Prayer

Let's pray: Oh Lord, teach me how to apply grace to my life. I want the grace that will allow me to love again, trust again, and try again. I have tried it my way, but I soon realized that my strength has expired. I need Your grace, the grace that covers my wrongs and gives me the power to do right. When I don't know how to, teach me how to function in Your grace, so that I too may boast in You. Lord, Your grace is sufficient enough for me. Thank You for not giving up on me, and as I grow in Your grace, continue to keep me and teach me. I am forever grateful. Amen.

Jot down thoughts in your *Capture the Moment Journal.*

Day 12

—

I Shall Recover All

The struggle is all too real in life when you have done all that you know how to do and yet it seems like you're losing more ground than you're gaining. You've taken two steps forward just to get knocked four steps back. How frustrating! However not all is lost, and even what was lost shall be recovered. The enemy can only go by what he sees; he does not possess the capacity to apply faith. When you begin to show signs of defeat, and you are consumed with the four steps you lost rather than the two steps that were gained, Satan responds to your reaction by rejoicing in what appears to be a victory. The story is not over; God can restore and cause you to recover all that was lost.

One Sunday afternoon my husband and I were watching a football game, and his team was losing by a huge margin. He could not bear to watch such a defeat, so he turned off the game before it was over. He focused on how many points his team was down; he never really considered the possibilities. The next day, as I was watching the news, the news anchor began to show highlights from the previous night's game, and to my surprise my husband's team had won. Apparently, they made a 61-yard pass, which caused them to recover and win the game. I called him to share the exciting news, but while speaking with him, he seemed disappointed.

"I would have loved to have seen the play by play action that lead to victory. I should've never turned off the television," he exclaimed.
Beloved, this is also true for your situation as well. Don't turn off or give up before the game is over! God wants you to know that regardless of what the score may be presently in your life, the game is not over. You shall recover all!

Our Focus Passage

1 Samuel 30:8 NLT
Then David asked the LORD, "Should I chase after this band of raiders? Will I catch them?" And the LORD told him, "Yes, go after them. You will surely recover everything that was taken from you!"

Let's talk about it.

Losing or having something stolen from you can be devastating. A divorce after 15 years of marriage, foreclosure on a home, a troubled teen, and the death of a loved one, bankruptcy, or a stolen car can cause you to feel violated and helpless. This is how David felt in 1 Samuel 30:8 when he returned home only to find devastation. The Amalekites burned their homes and took the women and children into captivity. In one day he lost everything. During those moments when loss, hopelessness and despair attempt to invade your thoughts and consume you, we must follow David's example and pray.

Once you take away fear and the disappointment of losing, or failing at something, your perspective of the outcome changes. The fear turns into confidence; the doubt turns into a possibility, weakness turns into strength, and the loss into gain! Deuteronomy 31:6 (NIV) explains it best: "Be strong and courageous. Do not be afraid or terrified because of them, for the LORD your God goes with you; he will never leave you nor forsake you."

Often we are so consumed with loss that we never consider the possibility of coming out of a situation victoriously. Experiencing loss can condition one not to ask or desire the things you used to request for the fear of losing again. Perhaps you are distraught over a relationship that ended. However, what you failed to realize is, instead of losing a relationship, you really lost your self-esteem, gentleness, and ability to love again. Despite your situation, I am here to announce to you that you shall recover all. You are recovering all of your joy, hope, confidence, strength, health, self-image, ambitions, and peace of mind. Often these are the first things we lose during crises, and yet during all the commotion you never file your insurance claim to recover what you truly lost. You did not even realize they had been lost; they were so easy to overlook because they are not tangible. However, they were the most valuable things.

Reflections:

- Take the time to seek God for instructions during an adverse situation. He is waiting to respond if you would only be willing to talk with Him. Pray.
- Don't focus on the tangible things you lost, as you might ignore what you truly lost, which are the unique things that make you who you really are, and not what the situation has caused you to become.

Stop and think about it.

Prayer

Let's pray: My Savior, thank You for being faithful and committed to my success and everything connected to me. I ask that You speak to me, instruct me, and guide me. Lord, I look to You, and trust that You will allow me to recover all! I thank You Lord that I am growing in the grace of God, and my understanding of Your ways. I give You praise, because Your grace will cause me to recover the joy, health, prosperity, hope, and peace that was lost or stolen. I stand on Your Word, which according to Psalms 84:11 states that You would not withhold any good thing from me. I wait patiently. Speak Lord and I will obey. Amen.

Jot down thoughts in your *Capture the Moment Journal.*

Day 13

—

Trust Him Even When You Can't See Him

We live in a culture where "seeing is believing." It is the ultimate proof that something happened or exists. You use your eyesight to guide you and to make decisions. This is why we watch for people's actions, because what they do is more believable than what they say. Although that is a good practice to implement, it can be deceiving when it's applied to God. He requires you to trust Him even when you can't see Him. You must believe His word above your own eyesight, because what you see will make you feel as if you are alone and defeated. Remember, "we walk by faith and not by sight" (2 Corinthians 5:7). He requires you to trust His voice to lead you through the dark and into the light.

Beloved, God not only sees what you are going through, but He will give you instructions on how to make it through. The storm was not sent to kill you but to make you stronger in your faith and in your relationship with Christ. Psalms 107:29 encourages us, declaring, "He caused the storm to be still, so that the waves of the sea were hushed." God will calm the waves that have been tossing you to and fro in your emotion. He will prove to your storm that He is in control. You need only to believe.

Our Focus Passage

Isaiah 25:4 (NLT)
But you are a tower of refuge to the poor, O LORD, a tower of refuge to the needy in distress. You are a refuge from the storm and a shelter from the heat.

Let's talk about it.

A storm is unpredictable. It may appear to be subsiding, but can turn worse in seconds. This is also true for the storms in your life. Wind, waves, and rain may make it nearly impossible to stay on course. You had great plans, hopes, and dreams before you were caught off-guard in a storm for which you were unprepared. Now that this storm has happened, you are afraid that you won't make it to shore, and that all will be lost. However, we have a glorious hope. Jesus, our Lord and King, is our Tower of Refuge, and our Refuge for the storm. In Isaiah, he mentions that Jesus our Lord is a refuge and shelter for four types of circumstances.

The first is a "tower of refuge to the poor." This means that in whatever area you are experiencing lack - financially, emotionally, or physically - He will be a tower shielding you from the effects of lack. The second one is "a tower of refuge to the needy in distress." This is God's promise to come to our aid when we are experiencing a crisis and need immediate help. It is no mistake that the first two places of refuge are described as a tower. Towers are lifted high above and are not easy to access. In the same way, God is declaring that not only will He hide you; He will elevate you above the situation, thus preventing lack and distress from having easy access to you and your family.

However, there are some storms in life that being lifted high would cause more harm than good. Consider a tornado. In that type of storm, it is safer to get underground. In the same way, God promises to be a refuge in whatever kinds of storms you encounter. He can protect you from the waves of a raging sea that's trying to overtake you, and the fierce winds of a hurricane attempting to destroy your peace and uproot you from your foundation, which is in Christ Jesus. Lastly, He will be a "shelter from the heat." This speaks of the exhaustion; sometimes the heat or pressure of life is too much to bear, and you just want relief. When you feel as if you're overwhelmed, and all your strength is gone, He will be a Shelter from the heat while giving you rest from your toil.

This is how mindful and concerned He is about you. He takes the time to encourage us in His Word. He knows that we encounter different storms and trials, but He promises in Psalms 34:19 t to deliver us from them all. You must trust and believe that when the storms of life appear to be overtaking you, know that God is with you! Isaiah 59:19 reminds us, "when the enemy comes in like a flood, The Spirit of the Lord will lift up a standard against him."

Reflections:
- God requires that we trust His Word more than what we see before us. If He told us that we were going to make it out of this, then regardless of what it looks like, we will make it out.
- Despite the strength of the storm that you are going through, God has already designed the appropriate type of refuge for your escape.

Stop and think about it.

Prayer

Let's pray: God, my strength and refuge in the time of trouble, I thank You for hiding me in Your presence. Help me to trust Your words when I can't see Your face. When I feel overwhelmed by life, be my shelter. Teach me to stand on Your words and rely on them to hold me up. I have tried everything else; now I give my storm over to You. I invite You into my situation. Thank you in advance for quieting my storm.

Jot down thoughts in your *Capture the Moment Journal.*

Day 14

—

Going Beyond Your Comfort Zone

To get what you want from God, you have to go beyond your comfort zone, beyond the familiar places and routines of life. He challenges us to step out in the deep waters, not to swim, but to walk on water. The drawback to stepping out is the false sense of security in the current situation. We confuse familiarity with safety because the situation can be predicted. Even if it's stressful and complicated, we trust it because it's familiar, and we do little to break free. A person will stay in an unhealthy relationship, a broken marriage, a stressful job, or live in an impoverished neighborhood, not because they enjoy their circumstances, but they fear the unknown should they decide to make a change.

Beloved, God never wanted you to blend in with the crowd and accept what life has handed you. He has called you to go beyond the stereotypes and press past your emotions and thrive! You were never designed to fit in with the crowd, but to stand out as a champion. This explains why you are so different from your family members. There is a buried desire deep within to go further, and you just need to know how to get it out. Well, God wants to dig up that buried desire and bring forth His glory in the earth through you. Yes, He wants to use you: the "not so perfect, wish I had more time, I just can't get it together" you. God has called you by name. Isaiah 45:3 (NTL) "And I will give you treasures hidden in the darkness - secret riches. I will do this so you may know that I am the LORD, the God of Israel, the one who calls you by name."

Our Focus Passage
Mark 4: 35-36 (NLT)
As evening came, Jesus said to his disciples, "Let's cross to the other side of the lake." 36 So they took Jesus in the boat and started out, leaving the crowds behind.

Let's talk about it.

In the verses before our focus passage, Jesus had just finished teaching and now He is giving the disciples instructions to go to the other side. God was pushing them and commanding them to go beyond what they knew. They wanted more from God, and the only way that they could experience it was to leave the shore and launch out into the deep. You also desire more from God, but it can't be received on the shore. You must go beyond the safety nets, the comfort of working for others, beyond your tax bracket, beyond coping and managing your pain, and beyond being normal and blending in.

In verse 36 it says, "they left the crowds behind." Often we want to take everybody with us because they are familiar. However, to get what is waiting on the other side, we must be willing to leave the crowds behind. You have to ignore people's negative opinions and any advice that is contrary to the promises of God for your life. You may have to leave behind friends or family who refuse to see beyond the drama of your past. This doesn't mean you don't love them or forgive them, but it does mean you have to limit their influence in your life and put God first.

The mere fact that you feel as if you are out here all alone, trusting God for a miracle marks you as one that is ready to go beyond. God wants you to face and conquer the fears tormenting your life. God wants you to confront the fear of rejection, the fear of not being good enough, fear of sickness, fear of loneliness, fear of failure, fear of dying, fear of repeated mistakes, and the fear of the unknown. Psalms 46:1 reminds us that, "God is our refuge and strength, an ever-present help in trouble." Although it's not easy and there are no visible guarantees that you are going to make it, don't lose hope. When you are afraid, seek the Lord, and He will get you safely to the other side!

Reflections:
- We walk by faith, as our sight can be deceiving. God's Word, which cannot be seen, is more powerful than things that can be seen.
- Leaving that comfort zone requires complete trust in God and in the promises He made. However, you must be willing to leave the crowds behind.

Stop and think about it.

Prayer

Let's pray: Dear God, I know that there is something deep down telling me there is more to me than being just average. You have great plans for me; please help me not to be afraid. I say yes to going above and beyond, and I ask for instructions on how You want me to do this because my understanding is limited. Show me how to leave the crowds behind, and to display the courage to face every fear. I am ready to go above and beyond for your glory. In Jesus name, Amen.

Jot down thoughts in your *Capture the Moment Journal.*

Day 15

—

Too Far Gone

God's mercies are new every morning, which gives us the opportunity to start again each day, to believe again, and thrive. Regardless of the number of mistakes or setbacks, God does not run out of mercies. Psalms 23:6 declares to us that, "Surely goodness and mercy shall follow me all the days of my life: and I will dwell in the house of the LORD forever." Because of His mercy and love, you can trust in the protection, provision, and peace as part of the household of faith. The word "follows" in Psalms 23:6, according to Strong's Concordance, means to chase, hunt, or to pursue. So God's love, and everything that comes with it, is chasing you down and waiting to pour out blessings, answers, help and provision. It will not stop until you have received the promises of God. We are reminded in Isaiah 40:8 that, "The grass withers and the flowers fall, but the word of our God endures forever."

Even with this knowledge, we often find it hard to believe that the situation will improve or will come to an end, nor that it will work out in our favor, or that God is a promise keeper. Sometimes, after praying, the circumstances or emotions get worse and we wonder if it's too far gone for God to resolve and restore the matter. My dear beloved, the situation is not dead, and it's far from being over; it is only asleep! God's Word will never fail. Matthew 24:35 assures us of this: "Heaven and earth will pass away, but my words will never pass away." You need only to believe because Heaven and earth will pass away before God's promise to you fails to come to pass!

Our Focus Passage

Luke 8:49-52 (NKJV)
49 While He was still speaking, someone came from the ruler of the synagogue's house, saying to him, "Your daughter is dead. Do not trouble the Teacher." 50 But when Jesus heard it, He answered him, saying, "Do not be afraid; only believe, and she will be made well." 51 When He came into the house, He permitted no one to go in except Peter, James, and John, and the father and mother of the girl. 52 Now all wept and mourned for her; but He said, "Do not weep; she is not dead, but sleeping."

Let's talk about it.

The ruler of the synagogue that our focus passage speaks of, is Jairus. Jairus, although a ruler, was just like everyone else; he had problems that only Jesus Christ could fix. In other words, he needed "Jesus to take the wheel" in this situation as his daughter's life depended on it. Much like Jairus, we need Jesus to come to our house and fix the problem! We have prayed and at one time believed; however, we became discouraged along the way. God knew we would get weak and become overwhelmed. He gave us hope in Isaiah 41:10: "Don't be afraid, for I am with you. Don't be discouraged, for I am your God. I will strengthen you and help you. I will hold you up with my victorious right hand." See, our hope and strength lies in Him, and even as a child takes the hand of their father and finds safety, we too can find safety and comfort in the hands of our Father.

As the story of Jairus continues in Luke 8:49, he receives devastating news that his daughter had died. Perhaps this is where you are in life; everything says that the situation is too far gone, and has progressed from being sick, to death. "Why do you continue to pray or believe? Why not just accept it?" the circumstances say. Yet, you have been chosen to be an example to all dying things; God has victory even over death through our Lord and Savior Jesus Christ! Revelation 1:18 (NLT) speaks of Christ's power over death. "I am the living one. I died, but look--I am alive forever and ever! And I hold the keys of death and the grave." The situation reported that she was dead. However, in verse 50, Jesus says, "Do not be afraid; only believe, and she will be made well." Although your situation appears to be dead, don't give up; it's only sleeping. There is nothing beyond God's reach, and although His timing might seem unfair, yet it is perfect. You need only to believe!

Reflections:

- The situation or issue is not beyond Christ's resurrection power. Even if it appears to have died, He can breathe life and cause it to live again.
- Don't be deceived by how long God takes to answer; just believe because, "All things are possible to them that believe!" (Mark 9:23)

Prayer

Let's pray: Father, we thank You for Your mercies that follow us when we make mistakes. We doubt and lose heart at times, but your love and goodness chases us. We trust You with the situation, and we are not moved by what we see, but trust we You through it all. We place our hand in Your hand of victory. We believe God, and we believe that Your promises are yea and amen. We believe in the impossible, because it becomes possible in your hands. Thank You God for giving me the strength to believe again.

Jot down thoughts in your *Capture the Moment Journal.*

Day 16

—

What Else Can Go Wrong?

While going through a difficult situation, the last thing you need is for something else to happen. You are tough and can handle most things, but the constant cycle of issues can weigh you down. You may be thinking to yourself, *"What else can go wrong?"* Peter encourages us in 1 Peter 4:12 by stating, "Dear friends, don't be surprised at the fiery trials you are going through as if something strange were happening to you."

My beloved, the suffering that you are experiencing "are not worthy to be compared with the glory which shall be revealed in us." [Roman 8:18 (KJV)] This is why you must not think it strange when you experience back-to-back trials, because God will get the glory out of your life. Yes, you have lost much for Christ's sake; however, God will restore. In Matthew 19:29 Jesus gives us a guarantee: "And everyone who has given up houses or brothers or sisters or father or mother or children or property, for my sake, will receive a hundred times as much in return and will inherit eternal life."

Our Focus Passage

2 Kings 4:1-2
One day the widow of a member of the group of prophets came to Elisha and cried out, "My husband who served you is dead, and you know how he feared the LORD. But now a creditor has come, threatening to take my two sons as slaves." 2"What can I do to help you?" Elisha asked. "Tell me, what do you have in the house?" "Nothing at all, except a flask of olive oil," she replied.

Let's talk about it.

In this passage, we are immediately made aware of the issue plaguing this woman, as the Bible refers to her as a widow. In Biblical times, a woman's identity was given up for her husband's, so to lose him was to lose more than a spouse. The widow's husband was the breadwinner, protector, and gave her access to things she would have been otherwise denied if she were not married. While attempting to cope with her recent loss, there's a knock at the door. It's the creditors threatening to take her sons away to make them slaves. Have you ever felt that if it's not one thing, it is another? However, despite the difficulty, you have what it takes in your possession to come out of every trial victorious. You have faith! 1 John 5:4 states: "For every child of God defeats this evil world, and we achieve this victory through our faith."

This woman was so entrenched in her trial that the Bible doesn't even record her name. Others appear to know her only by her issue, "the widow." Sometimes you feel as if you are known only as your issue. You are no longer Tina, Martha, or Tasha but you are known as debt, stress, irresponsible, bad luck with men, struggling mom, and used up. Although this is what your situation dictates to you, God has called you His bride, and with this marriage comes a name change. He changed your name from the issues to victory, delightful, pleasant, and beautiful (Song of Solomon 1:16). The prophet Elisha asked the widow "What do you have in your house?"

Christ is asking you the same question. *What's in your house? What's inside of you?* He left you a guarantee. 1 Corinthians 6:19 explains: "Don't you realize that your body is the temple of the Holy Spirit, who lives in you and was given to you by God? You do not belong to yourself." Just as the widow did not belong to herself but to her husband, you too belong to God. This means it is not your responsibility to work things out, but you were given power through the Holy Spirit. John 14:16 (Amp) states it best: "And I will ask the Father, and He will give you another Helper (Comforter, Advocate, Intercessor—Counselor, Strengthener, Standby), to be with you forever." You have a Helper during those times when you feel helpless. You have a Comforter within you, who is an Advocate to plead your case. He is an Intercessor to pray for you when everyone else forgets and a Counselor to give you instructions. The Holy Spirit is a strengthener to hold you up when you are weak, and He's the help waiting on standby to assist you wherever you need it. You have everything you need in your "house!"

Reflections:

- The widow didn't think that her oil was enough to get her through, but it was not how much oil she had; it was her faith that brought her out.
- You have something greater than oil inside of you; He is the Holy Spirit. Through Him, you will have access to total victory, complete joy, and unlimited provision.

Stop and think about it.

Prayer

Let's pray: Holy Spirit, I ask that You teach me how to access You in my time of trouble. I need You to teach me and guide me. Lord, comfort me in the places where I hurt. Be my advocate in the areas where I need someone to stand up for me. When I feel abandoned, stand by me, Holy Spirit. I yield to You, as these burdens are too much for me to bear. Help me. When I run out of words to pray, please intercede for me, Holy Spirit. Amen

Jot down thoughts in your *Capture the Moment Journal.*

Day 17

—

I Still Have a Smile On My Face!

God is truly faithful. When you consider all the ups and downs you've experienced, He has been faithful through it all. There are many that could not have survived the upbringing you had, the neighborhood you grew up in, or the losses you endured. Yet, you have persevered through life's challenges and you've overcome some of your greatest fears. The scriptures describe it in Romans 8:37(NIV): "in all these things we are more than conquerors through him who loved us."

You have fought and won many battles, and you're left with the scars of war. However, those battle scars are now a testimony of how He brought you out. He makes us a promise in Psalms 34:19 (NIV): "The righteous person may have many troubles, but the LORD delivers him from them all."

Beloved, you must have a firm understanding that the Lord fights on your behalf and secures every victory. With this newfound confidence you can walk with your head held high, and despite your troubles, you can say, "I still have a smile on my face!"

Our Focus Passage
Exodus 15:2 (NIV)
"The LORD is my strength and my defense; he has become my salvation. He is my God, and I will praise him, my father's God, and I will exalt him."

Let's talk about it.

Throughout this devotional, the focus has been on scriptures that speak of God's love and promises to His children. However, this particular passage starts with a declaration of who God is. The children of Israel just witnessed a miracle; God parted the Red Sea and destroyed the Egyptians. In one day what had oppressed and enslaved them was utterly destroyed. Moses told the people to stand still and see the salvation of God, as He would prove to their enemy that they were more than conquerors. You too must know that it's not your fight nor is it your responsibility to prove anything to your enemy. Although the circumstances you're facing are much bigger and stronger than you, God says you do not have to be afraid. Consider Deuteronomy 3:22: "Do not be afraid of them; the LORD your God himself will fight for you." Because the Lord fights for you, when you're weak you can declare with confidence, "The Lord is my strength!"

Those who trust in God will never lose or be put to shame. Romans 10:11 states, "Anyone who believes in him will never be put to shame." Much like the children of Israel, you started off with a promise from God. Now everything around you declares, "Give up, you're too weak" and mocks you because you have decided to wait on God. I am reminded of the passage in Psalms 20:7, which states: "Some trust in chariots and some in horses, but we trust in the name of the LORD our God."

Anytime you believe God for bigger and better things, those who oppress you or desire for you to be defeated will mock your belief. Perhaps it's the successful family member, who did everything perfectly, laughs when you, the imperfect one, share that you want to be a business owner someday. Maybe it's that friend who can't bear being alone, so they discourage any form of happiness in your life. It may be the paycheck that torments you and reminds you that you don't make enough when you have goals of being debt free, and the ability to travel. Regardless of who or what is mocking you, continue to make your boast in the Lord.

You will be able to declare before the end of the thing, "The LORD is my strength and my defense" and boast on how He has become your salvation! See, salvation doesn't stop at merely accepting Jesus as Savior and Lord, but continues to save in every area of your life. Just when they thought surely, she will give up now that things have gotten worst, your Hero, Jesus, comes in and saves the day. He is your God, so while others frown, let your smile testify of His goodness.

Reflections:
- I do not have to fight my battles because God fights for me.
- I am confident in God's strength and abilities not my own.
- Whatever had me bound will have to let me go because God has made me free.

Let's declare: God You are my strength, my helper, my defense, my hope, my peace, my joy, my champion, my victory, my encouragement, my friend, my sustainer, my rock, and my answer. I am confident in Your strength and abilities and not my own. I will not be moved by those who mock me because I believe and trust You. When no one else believes, I will encourage myself in You Lord, for You are my confidence. I will remain resilient and steadfast in the face of doubt and opposition. I will persevere and overcome the obstacles designed to stop me. You are my help in the time of trouble and You will hide me in Your presence. You are faithful, and it is because of Your faithfulness that I can declare that I am more than a conqueror. I win in every area of my life. I win in my finances, in my health, in my emotions, and in my mind. Amen.

Jot down thoughts in your *Capture the Moment Journal.*

Day 18

—

God Will Cause Me To Laugh

In John chapter 5, a disabled man was lying next to a pool called Bethesda for 38 years, waiting to be healed. He was not alone in his pursuit of healing. The Bible describes in John 5:3 that there "lay a great multitude of sick people..." The man desired to be healed but when the water was troubled someone always got in the water before him. Have you ever experienced a helpless feeling? You know what you need to do to resolve the matter, but you just don't have the strength or the means to do it. This makes you feel paralyzed by your circumstances.

Beloved, Jesus can come to where you are and give you guidance, strength, and instructions that will change your life forever. The man at the pool was waiting for someone to HELP him to get in the water, but Jesus gave him instructions that would heal every space of his life. You too have been waiting for someone or something to help you get out of this mess, where everything you've tried has failed. Regardless of how long you have been in that state, or how many times you failed, God will cause you to laugh in victory over your sorrows.

Our Focus Passage

Psalms 126:2
Our mouths were filled with laughter, our tongues with songs of joy. Then it was said among the nations, "The LORD has done great things for them."

Let's talk about it.

Although you might not see it or even believe it, you will look back at all your troubles, disappointments, heartbreaks, and laugh! The pain will have no effect, and the tears of sorrow will turn into tears of joy. Your laughter will be a witness of the great things that the Lord will do for you and your family. I love how the focus passages states, "your mouth will be filled with laughter." This means that there will be no more room for complaining, arguing, or negative words - only laughter! Your laughter will announce to the world that God is faithful and is a Restorer of lost time.

When God answers prayers, the pain of the trial is forgotten. Abraham and Sarah had a promise from God; He promised them a son. However, they did not believe it could happen, and instead, they laughed at God (Genesis 17:17). Whether you or others are laughing in disbelief, God's Word will not falter. He has a way of turning midnight into day, tears of sorrow into tears of joy, and a cynical laugh into a celebration of laughter.

In the Bible, Job lost everything dear to him, yet he testified in Job 8:21 that "He will yet fill your mouth with laughter and your lips with shouts of joy." Job was tested in every area: family, death, loss of wealth, marital issues, friends walking away, health challenges, and a ruined reputation, yet he too was able to laugh again. God wants you to get ready to laugh at all those moments you doubted and when others waited to laugh at your demise. Job 5:22 says, "You will laugh at destruction and famine, and need not fear the wild animals."

God is getting ready to make up for the struggles in your life, and cause people to join in with you in celebrating what God has done. The promise seems too good to be true, but God's power thrives in the impossible. So laugh! Fill your mouth with laughter and songs of praise for your promises are on the way. Then, all the nations we declare, "The Lord has done great things."

Reflections:

- The moment in life that brought you sorrow, God will cause you to laugh in victory.
- Those who are waiting to see if God will deliver you will join you in celebration of God's faithfulness.

Stop and think about it.

Let's declare: God, I will not be afraid of the things that I am facing, but You, oh Lord, will cause me to laugh in the face of my enemy. I will laugh at my troubles and remember them no more. I will open up my mouth wide and declare your praise, for You have brought me from a small place into a large place. Psalms 18:19 states that You have "brought me out into a spacious place; he rescued me because he delighted in me." You are not limited to time or people but You will restore the time that I have lost and grant me favor. I will achieve every goal; I will experience healing and deliverance. You will never withhold any good thing from me. I am blessed and highly favored among women, and I have been chosen by God to excel! So I will laugh and remain in the joy of the Lord, for it is my strength.

Jot down thoughts in your *Capture the Moment Journal.*

Day 19

—

I Got This!

Take a moment to reflect. After all you have experienced, you know without a shadow of doubt that you are resilient, fearless, and an overcomer. What held you down before will be the same thing that God uses to lift you up and propel you into the next dimension of your life. God doesn't waste anything; He uses everything to produce His glory and favor in your life. This is why the scripture states in Romans 8:28: "And we know that all things work together for good to them that love God, to them who are the called according to his purpose." Even the dark and dim chapters of life help complete your story.

Beloved, now that you've tasted victory, there is no turning back for you. You can look at challenges and setbacks and say, "I got this!" You can believe God for bigger, wider, and deeper things and stand firm until you see it come to pass. You are not trusting in your own strength, but you have learned to lean on God and in His abilities and resources. You trust His Word every step of the way, and you're acknowledging Him in all your ways.

Our Focus Passage

Joshua 2:24 NKJV
"And they said to Joshua, "Truly the Lord has delivered all the land into our hands, for indeed all the inhabitants of the country are fainthearted because of us."

Just like you, the children of Israel believed that God would bring His promises to pass, which was the land flowing with milk and honey, a place they could call their own. In Numbers 13:2 The Lord commanded Moses to "Send some men to explore the land of Canaan, which I am giving to the Israelites." The Lord did not ask them to fight; God said, "I am giving" them the land. All that was required of them was to receive. The Lord is not asking you to fight either. He has already made the way; you just need to receive.

We are so accustomed to working and fighting for what we have that it's hard to grasp the concept of just receiving. Jeremiah 1:12 (ESV) states: "for I am watching over my word to perform it." The Lord removes the burden of working for it, and He takes on the responsibility of making sure it comes to pass. He desires for His children to do three things: believe, relax, and receive. The Lord wants you to believe that He can do it, relax because He has it all under control, and receive His blessings with open arms.

In Numbers 13:31 the spies came back with this report stating, "But the men who had gone up with him said, "We can't attack those people; they are stronger than we are." How often do you think along those lines? Perhaps you thought to yourself: *Is God crazy? I can't do this.* Yet, God never once asked you to use your strength and resources to get it done. Proverbs 5:7 suggests that you "Commit your works to the LORD and your plans will be established." In other words, allow God to take away the burden of working, and watch Him make it happen. Which brings us to our focus passage, Joshua 2:24.

Joshua sent out two spies, and their report was different from the initial twelve spies whom Moses sent out. The two spies' report stated, "The LORD has surely given the whole land into our hands." You can make your boast in the Lord, knowing that He fights for you and places victory in your hand. Proverbs 21:30 states: "There is no wisdom, no insight, no plan that can succeed against the LORD." Because the Lord has guaranteed victory, you can look at your toughest challenge and say, "I got this." Remember that the ten spies reported that they were not strong enough; however, the two spies reported that the inhabitants of the land were terrified because of them. God changed their fear into a testimony of greatness. The God is turning things you didn't feel strong enough to defeat into a testimony. Lack, depression, hate, sickness, death and loneliness will tremble at the sight of you, and you will possess your promised land.

Reflections:
- As a good Father, He takes on that burden and ensures that His word comes to pass.
- You can have confidence in knowing that your God fights for you and places the victory in your hands.
- Your testimony is changing from fearing to being feared by the enemies that occupy your promised land.

Stop and think about it.

Let's declare: The Lord has granted me victory over my enemies. I no longer see myself as weak or defeated, but I see a champion. When I look at myself, I see strength and victory. I remove the limitation that I place on my emotions and mental state. I can and will love again, believe again, start again, and pursue again. I no longer fear failure or shame, but shame and failure will fear me. I walk boldly in the promises of God and receive all that He has promised me with open arms. Doubt and unbelief are far from me and I believe all things and I can do all things. I will possess every promise that God has given to me.

Jot down thoughts in your *Capture the Moment Journal.*

Day 20

—

I Win!

We have all heard the term, "winning isn't everything." However, to a person who has suffered countless losses, a win means the world. Hannah (Samuel 1:1-28) had experienced countless losses as year after year she attempted to bear a child with no success. However, Hannah experienced a single win that would change her life and generations to come; she gave birth to Samuel. God had already heard Hannah's plea the first time she prayed, yet the pregnancy was for an appointed time. We must understand that it's not about winning every time, but winning at the right time. Ecclesiastes 3:1 reminds us, "There is a time for everything and a season for every activity under the heavens."

Beloved, I want you to know that it is your time to win! Although you were the underdog and voted the least likely to succeed, you are getting reading to experience a win in your life that will affect generations to come. The time is right and the season of losing has ended. You have entered the season of I Win! The vision that God has for you will manifest and speak, declaring you as an undefeated champion. Habakkuk 2:3 (NLT) states: "This vision is for a future time. It describes the end, and it will be fulfilled. If it seems slow in coming, wait patiently, for it will surely take place. It will not be delayed."

Our Focus Passage

John 16:33 (NIV)
"I have told you these things so that in me you may have peace. In this world, you will have trouble. But take heart! I have overcome the world."

Let's talk about it.

When Christ died on the cross, His disciples thought all was lost. However, what they considered a loss was the ultimate WIN that would grant victory for all humanity. The circumstances and conditions that have been plaguing your family will be defeated by the cross you bear. 2 Timothy 2:12 states "If we suffer, we shall also reign with him..." Since Christ endured loss in order to gain, you too will endure, but produce an everlasting victory for generations to come.

The disciples thought that death was the end of Jesus. However, Christ proved that death was no match for Him. Your circumstances may look like the end, but just as Christ did, you will rise out of this with all power! 1 Corinthians 6:14 declares, "By his power, God raised the Lord from the dead, and he will raise us also." Death could not hold down our Savior, and it will not hold you down. Rise, and again I say, rise out of the ashes of death, shame, and defeat and claim your victory.

When you are at your weakest moment, you are your strongest! Paul suffered greatly, but expressed his testimony in 2 Corinthians 12:10 which states, "That is why, for Christ's sake, I delight in weaknesses, in insults, in hardships, in persecutions, in difficulties. For when I am weak, then I am strong." Beloved, you must understand that if God is for you, who or what can be against you (Romans 8:31)? In this world, we will have trouble, but the good news is Jesus has overcome the world! In other words, He has overcome addictions, disappointments, betrayal, sickness, anger, mistreatment, lies, hatred, abandonment, lack, jealousy, and loneliness. Jesus endured all things, so that we may experience victory in all things.

You will not obtain the win by works or doing everything right; however, you shall prevail because you belong to God. Galatians 4:7 states: "So you are no longer a slave, but God's child; and since you are his child, God has made you also an heir." We are no longer slaves to defeat and despair, but heirs to the King of kings. If a man is rich by default, his children are rich and have access to all the benefits that come with being the child of a rich man. The child did nothing to earn it, yet because they bear the same last name, it allows the child to receive the fruits of his father's labor. You have worked and labored long enough; it is time to receive. Experience the benefits that come with being a child of the Most High God. He has guaranteed your victory; you win.

Reflections:

- Because Christ has overcome the world, you too are an overcomer.
- You are joint heirs with Christ, which gives you access to the benefits of being a child of the King.
- You win! Not by power or might but simply because you belong to God.

Stop and think about it.

Let's declare: I am a champion. Failure and defeat are far from me, and my house. I am victorious because the Lord fights for me and He has won. I triumph over my problems and destroy the obstacles that rise against me. I am victorious over my past, and I am a champion in my future. I do not live in regret, nor do I wallow in sorrow, but I will persevere against the odds and I will prevail over my enemies. I am brave, strong, courageous, gallant, undefeated through Christ, and a child of God. I win in my finances, my emotions, my health, in relationships, and in every area concerning my family and me. I am more than a conqueror; I win.

Jot down thoughts in your *Capture the Moment Journal.*

It's GO Time.

In Leviticus 14:2 (NLT) the children of Israel received strict instructions for those healed of leprosy. It stated: "The following instructions are for those seeking ceremonial purification from a skin disease. Those who have been healed must be brought to the priest." God wants you to know you are healed and you can show yourself to the High Priest, who is our Lord and Savior, Christ Jesus. You no longer have to hide in shame, for the Lord has declared you cleansed and whole. Now that you're made whole, God is challenging you to step out on faith and put it into action. Every person whom Jesus healed, He required immediate action and would make statements such as, "Go and sin no more," "Take up your bed and walk," "Go, your faith has made you whole," or "Go and wash."

It's time to take action and "GO!" There are "GO" challenges at the end of each daily reflection. These GO challenges are putting action to your faith and demonstrating to those around you that you are mended and Christ has made you whole.

Day 21

—

Fearless

Is life bullying you? The situation you face is intimidating, as it is bigger and stronger than you. For instance, the medical bills are bigger than your bank account, or that person's stubbornness is stronger than the love you're trying to give. David, in the Bible, understood this feeling very well as he too had to encounter and confront a bully. The bully's name was Goliath, a skilled warrior in the Philistine army. David, at that time, was a shepherd boy and had no experience in war or battle tactics. He was not a warrior but a humble shepherd. The odds were against David in every way. Let's compare: David was a shepherd and Goliath was a warrior. David was a boy and Goliath was an experienced adult trained in the art of war. Goliath had a sword and armor; David had lunch, a slingshot, and his faith in God.

Despite the odds, David understood one very important thing and recorded it in Psalms 27:1 (NIV): "The LORD is my light and my salvation - whom shall I fear? The LORD is the stronghold of my life - of whom shall I be afraid?" He recognized that the Lord was on his side, which caused David to be fearless in the face of his enemies. My beloved, I'm not sure what bullies you are facing in life, but I do know that the Lord is your light in a dark place; a stronghold, and your salvation, so whom or what shall you fear?

Our Focus Passage

Psalms 112:7-8 (NLT)
They do not fear bad news; they confidently trust the LORD to care for them.
They are confident and fearless and can face their foes triumphantly.

Let's talk about it.

Consider the story of David and Goliath; we can see how the Lord caused David to prevail. Often times we can look at the Bible characters and feel as if they had some type of superpower. They slew giants, survived the lion's den and walked in fiery furnaces. However, if you examine closely, there is a common thread that the Bible characters shared, which was fearlessness. It was not that they had no fear of what was to come or the situation. They chose not to consider what could be lost in the situation, and focused on what could be gained. They did not fear losing their lives, friends, status, or money if it meant that Jesus' name would be glorified.

God wants you to realize that you have nothing to lose, but everything to gain. Facing your fear makes you fearless. According to Matthew 16.25 (NIV): "For whoever wants to save their life will lose it, but whoever loses their life for me will find it." In other words, when you're more concerned about saving your reputation, image, or protecting your pride, the very thing you tried to avoid will become a reality. If God told you to start it, try again, or be still, you must not let the fear of losing control grip you. When you are willing to let go of the fear of losing, you will realize that you have grabbed onto hope and courage, and you have become fearless. In our focus passage, Psalms 112:7, it explains that you don't have to fear bad news, but you can be confident that the Lord will work it out for your good.

The bad news is never the final report or outcome, but know that the Lord fights for you and never loses. You must run out to confront those fears, just as David ran to meet Goliath, and stand firm on the promises of God.
It is just a shadow of death. King David explains in Psalms 23 it is not death itself. Don't fear what could happen if you trust again, or what they will say about you if you choose to step out on faith. Psalms 112:8 explains it this way: "They are confident and fearless and can face their foes triumphantly." No more hiding or avoiding your fears. This is your moment to stand up and become fearless.

Reflections:

- Fearlessness doesn't mean the absence of fear, but the choice to confront your fears despite the situation and outcome.
- You don't have to fear bad news, but you can have confidence in knowing that Christ is with you and He will rescue you.
- You're not going through this to lose, but to gain. If you try to save it with your own strength, it will be lost, yet when you remove the fear of loss, you will gain what God has promised.

The "GO" Challenge:

1.   It's time to confront your Goliath. Confront whatever has kept you from believing, trusting, trying, starting, doing, or completing what God has promised and/or instructed and include it in your Capture the Moment Journal.

2.   It's time to gather five smooth stones that you will use to defeat your Goliath (fear). List five things that will assist you in defeating your giant (fears) in your **Capture the Moment journal**.

Confession:
Philippians 4:13 NIV
I can do all things through Christ which strengthens me.

Day 22

—

You Have Something To Give

As we grow in the grace of God, we find ourselves in moments of reflection, thinking: "If I only knew what I know now, I would be further along in life." Yet, every cracked, shattered, and broken piece in your life has made you who you are. You are resilient, wiser and stronger than ever before. Now that you are experiencing victory, it's time to share your testimony so that others may experience victory. Revelation 12:11 explains that, "we overcome by the word of our testimony," so without a testimony how can one overcome? You must begin to tell others of the goodness of Jesus, so that they too may partake in the victory. You might not have achieved your ultimate goals or feel as if you have a long way to go before you can help someone else. This is not true, and the more you give out, the more the Lord gives back to you.

Consider the story of Ruth and Naomi, her mother-in-law. Ruth, Orpah, and Naomi had lost their husbands, and Naomi felt as if she had nothing else to offer Ruth and her sister. Ruth 1:12 NIV records Naomi's response: "Return home, my daughters; I am too old to have another husband." In other words, "I have suffered loss, and I have no way of fixing your problem while I am currently facing my own." Naomi encourages them to go back home and because of her issues, little did Naomi know that the Lord would use her greatly to guide Ruth into her destiny. Just like Naomi, my beloved, you have something to give! Naomi shared her wisdom, which helped Ruth go from gleaning and picking up scraps in the field to becoming the owner of the field. Ruth overcame by Naomi's testimony.

Our Focus Passage
Proverbs 31:9 (NLT)
She extends a helping hand to the poor and opens her arms to the needy.

Let's talk about it.

The true test of deliverance and maturity is to be strong enough to go back and rescue someone in a lower state than you. The Proverbs 31 woman was not great only because of her own value but her greatness was reflected in her ability to value others through service. The focus passage points out that she "extends a helping hand." She did not help in the areas of convenience, but stretched past her comfort zone while extending her resources, time, and efforts to those with less. It does not indicate if the Proverbs 31 woman had a great deal of wealth, but what she had in her hand she gave it to help others.

This speaks of a sacrifice, which was a reflection of the sacrifice that Jesus Christ made so that all might be saved. Maybe someone in your church or community is suffering from a lack of joy, peace, or hope. You can extend and stretch yourself to give them a word of encouragement, a hug that will comfort them, or a smile that lets them know there is still hope. Proverbs 19:17 (NLT) says, "If you help the poor, you are lending to the LORD--and he will repay you!" What you give out is not lost, but the Lord promises to repay you for your good deeds. You can never run out of the resource you chose to give back. As you give, you make space for God to fill you with more!

Beloved, our Lord, and Savior, Jesus Christ, sees your plight and is not blind to the fact that you are still encountering struggles. However, He is teaching you to live as He lived by helping those less fortunate than yourself. Naomi did not have to help Ruth, but when she did she was blessed in the midst and experienced restoration. As you are on the journey of getting healed and delivered, pick up someone along the way and extend a helping hand. You can no longer stay confined and live behind a wall of protection. Once you give to others, it pours healing oil on the wounds of your heart and causes you to experience restoration and hope. Consider Deuteronomy 15:10 (NIV): "Give generously to them and do so without a grudging heart; then because of this the LORD your God will bless you in all your work and in everything you put your hand to." Hallelujah! When you give hope, God will cause you to overflow in it.

Reflections:
- You don't have to wait to accomplish your goals or have victory in an area of your life before you can be a blessing to someone else.
- No matter how much you extend a helping hand, God is there waiting to give back what you gave and more.

Your "GO" Challenge:

You are Naomi, but who will be your Ruth? In your *Capture the Moment journal*, list someone or a local organization that you will volunteer your time and extend efforts to help, e.g. mentor a youth on your block, serve at a homeless shelter, babysit for a single mom, or visit the elderly.

Confession:

Luke 6:38 (NLT)

"Give, and you will receive. Your gift will return to you in full - pressed down, shaken together to make room for more, running over, and poured into your lap. The amount you give will determine the amount you get back."

Day 23

—

Speak Life

God has given us a very powerful tool called hope. It gives us the power to believe when all appears to be lost, and it helps us to thrive during barren circumstances. Hope is like a muscle; it gives you the strength you need to push or pull your way through adversity. In the gym, only resistance and moving heavy weight strengthens muscle. This is also true about hope. The resistance you've encountered through rejection, or through the heavy burdens you bear, strengthens your hope. Everyone likes the results of the workout, but hates the process of the workout. The process stretches your capabilities, tests your limits, and challenges your current physical condition. Life is the workout, and the Holy Spirit is the Trainer, helping you strengthen hope, your muscle.

Beloved, when your muscle begins to lose strength, you hear the Holy Spirit, the Trainer, say words such as, "You are more than a conqueror (Rom 8:37)," "Weeping may endure for a night but joy is coming (Ps 30:5)," or, "You can do all things through Christ (Phil 4:13)," which builds up your faith. Those few words speak life into your muscles, causing you to lift, push, pull, or endure the pain and reach your goal.

Our Focus Passage
Ezekiel 37:3-5 (NLT)
Then he asked me, "Son of man, can these bones become living people again?" "O Sovereign LORD," I replied, "you alone know the answer to that." (4) Then he said to me, "Speak a prophetic message to these bones and say, 'Dry bones, listen to the word of the LORD! (5) This is what the Sovereign LORD says: Look! I am going to put breath into you (dry bones) and make you live again!

Let's talk about it.

The Lord had made a promise to restore His people. He began to speak to the prophet Ezekiel concerning a valley of bones (Ezekiel 37:1). The prophet in verse 2 confirms that there were a great number of bones and that they were "completely dried out." There were too many bones to count and they had been dead for quite some time, far beyond the point of even hoping for life. They were scattered, broken, and dried out. Why would the Lord ask, "Can these bones live?" Have you considered that the Lord was not asking a question, but He was instead demonstrating how the Israelites felt about their own situation? In the same way, the Lord is revealing your heart and your thoughts regarding the circumstances that you have been facing.

God made you a promise, but all you can see is a valley of dead bones. What are these dead bones, you may ask? They are scattered promises, broken dreams, and potential that you thought had died. The Lord wants you to know that despite how dried out the dead bones are, or regardless of how much time has passed, there is always hope. Hope will cause those dead bones to live again. He can bring them to pass right before your eyes.

Speak the words of life over the dead bones you see. What did God say? What did he promise? What did He show you? God's Word is more real than anything you can see, smell, or touch; it is the very essence of life. In the focus passage, the Lord tells you what is going to happen when you speak His words. He says in verse 5 of Ezekiel 37: "Look! I am going to put breath into you (dead bones) and make you live again!"

Those dreams are not over and the time has not been wasted, for God wastes nothing. The time was just resistance training to strengthen your hope. The weight you had to lift and carry for so many years built up your endurance and increased your faith. Now your hope is stronger and you can lift and endure more. You can also share Abraham's testimony, recorded in Romans 4:18 (NIV) which states: "Against all hope, Abraham in hope believed and so became the father of many nations, just as it had been said to him." He hoped against the odds, and hoped against the lack of hope and he became what our Heavenly Father intended. Yes, these dry bones will live!

Reflections:
- The Lord is using this situation to strengthen your faith and hope in Him so that you can overcome in areas of life that appear dead.
- It is God's words that carry the power to give life, so you must speak what He has said so you can see a change in your circumstances.

Your "GO" Challenge:

What has God promised you about the situation you're facing? Write the promises in your *Capture the Moment Journal*, and just as the Lord had Ezekiel speak to the dry bones, declare God's words of life over the bones of your promise.

Confession:

Lord I thank You for changing my heart regarding the situation that I am facing. Where I once saw death, I now see life. Lord You have mended my heart, and now words of life are springing forth from my mouth. Thank You for causing me to live again and dream again.

Day 24

—

I Am Whole

Have you ever purchased an item from the store and realized, once you got home, that it was broken or damaged? Once you discovered the merchandise was broken, the thrill and excitement of the purchase was immediately extinguished. However, God has a difference of opinion on damaged goods. Beloved, people see the flaws in your life, the cracks, bumps and bruises. Yet, God sees His Son's blood that covers every broken and flawed place.

The Lord does not discard you because of a flaw, nor does He value you any less because of it. His love is unconditional, faithful, and consistent. God's love never fails. He has purchased you, as you were bought with a price; the blood of Jesus Christ redeemed you. However, He won't return you or ask for His money back, no matter how damaged you may appear to be. God plays a dual role in this mending process, as He is the Purchaser and the Manufacturer. The Lord fashioned you in His image and knew everything about you and how you work. With each product, he created He has given a 100% satisfaction guarantee, and will right the wrongs and repair the broken.

Our Focus Passage

Luke 8:43-44 (NKJV)
Now a woman, having a flow of blood for twelve years, who had spent all her livelihood on physicians and could not be healed by any, came from behind and touched the border of His garment. And immediately her flow of blood stopped.

Let's talk about it.

During those times a woman with her condition was considered unclean (Leviticus 15:25) and it was against the law for her to be in the city or among people. Not only was she considered unclean; everything she touched was considered unclean. The woman could have been stoned to death for breaking the law; however, it was a risk that she was willing to take. Drained and weak from 12 years of blood lost, she still believed that her condition was not permanent. Her issues had isolated her long enough; she wanted to experience life again. She put a demand on the anointing that granted her access to Jesus' saving power.

You too have been considered unclean, according to the law of man, so you stop going to church and you've isolated yourself from those who love you. You are spending all that you have, trying to appease the pain of being unclean. You buy a bigger house, make more money, or go from relationship to relationship just to realize, *"I am still unclean."* God is not afraid of contamination nor is He concerned about others' opinions of you. Instead, He longs for you to reach out and touch Him. The woman with the issue of blood remained persistent in her pursuit of being healed and made whole. Matthew 7:7 (NLT) explains it this way; "Keep on asking, and you will receive what you ask for. Keep on seeking, and you will find. Keep on knocking, and the door will be opened to you."

In our focus passage Luke 8:43 (NKJV) it states: "Now a woman, having a flow of blood for twelve years, who had spent all her livelihood on physicians and could not be healed by any." She tried everything, and so have you. However, there is still hope. You might have to press through a crowd while enduring the shame. You will have to overcome your fears and people's opinions to touch Jesus, but it is so worth it! You will be made whole and peace will flood your life.

Reflections:

- No matter how long you have endured the circumstance, condition, or pain, when you connect with Jesus, even if others deem you unworthy, you will be made whole.
- God is not intimidated by your problems nor is He concerned about how others feel about your unclean situation. His blood is there to heal you and make you clean.
- Keep knocking and seeking until God opens that door to your miracle. Never give up. This is your year to overcome and be victorious.

Your "GO" Challenge:

The woman with the issue of blood had to press through the crowd to receive her miracle from Jesus. What are some of the things you need to press through, get over, or conquer to receive what you are believing God for? Write them in your *Capture the Moment Journal*. Then, ask God to strengthen your hope and increase your faith so you can "GO" and receive your miracle from Jesus.

Confession:

Yes, I have issues, but I will no longer let them define me. I will no longer be known as the woman with the issue of blood, but the woman who is whole! I am healed, forgiven, and loved. I will not let my past hold me captive, but I will break free and become what I was destined to be. I will endure and overcome my issues and people's opinions to get what I need from God. Even in my unclean state, I will not allow my mistakes to keep me from God's love and mercy. I come boldly to His throne while ignoring the tradition of man. I am bathing in His unwavering love for me. I am receiving the help that I need, while allowing the Holy Spirit to mend every broken piece and fill every empty space. I am whole.

Day 25

—

I'm Not Cocky; I'm Confident

When a woman believes in herself, she is instantly labeled as cocky. There seems to be no middle ground. You either have low self-esteem or you are stuck up. This scenario reminds me of the story of Queen Vashti in the book of Esther, chapter one. Contrary to popular teaching that she was an un-submissive wife, I admire the courage of Queen Vashti. The story began when King Xerxes hosted a banquet to show off his kingdom and riches. During the feast, verse 10 records that king Xerxes was "merry with wine" and was now requesting the presence of his Queen, Vashti. Esther 1:11 (NIV) records the event: "to bring before him Queen Vashti, wearing her royal crown, in order to display her beauty to the people and nobles, for she was lovely to look at."

Although at first glance it appears Vashti is cocky, as she refused the king's wishes. However, that was not the case; Vashti knew her worth and refused to be exploited for her beauty and treated like an object. She refused to let anyone devalue her worth, even if that person was the King. Queen Vashti was not cocky, but confident and did not need men to admire her body or compliment her beauty to establish self-worth. My beloved, now that you are discovering the new you, people will automatically assume that you think highly of yourself. When they attempt to insult you by calling you cocky, respond in this way: I'm not cocky, I'm confident.

Our Focus Passage
Hebrew 10:35 (NLT)
So do not throw away this confident trust in the Lord. Remember the great reward it brings you!

Let's talk about it.

Once God restores you and brings you into remembrance of who you truly are, there is a newness that comes with it: a new attitude, a different thought process, perspective, and greater confidence. You no longer see the rejected, broken, and bruised little girl, but you see royalty and prestige. You are confident in your new royal attire, and you refuse to bow to anything that resembles the garments of a peasant. However, people and circumstances attempt to remind you of the peasant garment you once wore. Jesus experienced this firsthand, and although He was the Messiah, people kept reminding Him that He was just the son of a carpenter. Although He performed miracle after miracle, the people attacked His confidence and refused to acknowledge who He was. Mark 6:3 (NIV) states: "Isn't this the carpenter? Isn't this Mary's son and the brother of James, Joseph, Judas and Simon? Aren't his sisters here with us?" And they took offense at him." This is your newfound reality, as others grew up seeing you depressed, lonely, overlooked, and victimized. They cannot accept the joyful, forgiven, delivered, healed and confident you.

Our focus passage states, "So do not throw away this confident trust in the Lord." in other words, just because people don't see it, agree with it, or believe, doesn't mean it's not true. You must not look for confirmation of your victory through the report of others, but you must trust in the Lord. They might not ever see you mended, and repeatedly bring up the scars of your past, but it does not change the truth that your faith has made you whole! When you have submitted to His divine plans, there is a confidence in knowing that there is a reward for all the sacrifice and heartache you had to endure. Hebrew 11:6 explains it in this way: "... he rewards those who earnestly seek him."

You have sought the Lord, purchased this book, and now you are taking a leap of faith to receive your breakthrough from God. The Bible is clear: Never throw your confidence away just because others see it as trash. God is getting the glory out of your life and your reward is great. He confirms this in Philippians 1:6 (NIV) which states: "being confident of this, that he who began a good work in you will carry it on to completion until the day of Christ Jesus." Remember, you are not cocky, but confident in the fact that He who started the good work in you will complete it.

Reflections:

- Although things and situations come, we must never throw away our confidence that God has forgiven, saved, and healed us, despite what others or we think.
- Just because others cannot see the healing and transformation that God has done in your life, it does not mean that it did not happen.

Your "GO" Challenge:

In your *Capture the Moment Journal*, identify and list some of the areas in your life where you have allowed people or circumstances to devalue you or strip you of your confidence. What did you learn from it and how will you prevent it from happening again?

Confession:

I am confident in who and what God says that I am. I will not allow my circumstances to dictate my emotions. I will look through the lenses of Christ, and accept forgiveness and love. I am valuable and deserve to be treated as such. I am humble because I know that it is by the Blood of Jesus Christ that I am who I am.

Day 26

—

It's Worth Every Tear

Once a woman goes into labor, the pain becomes unbearable as she prepares to give birth. With tears of agony flowing down her cheeks, she just wants it to be over. The ice chips aren't helping, and the backrubs are of no effect. The discomfort and emotions begin to take their toll until that unforgettable moment happens. The baby is born and she instantly forgets about the discomfort and pain as she holds the baby in her arms.

Beloved, it's not easy to believe and trust again, but it is worth it. Much like an expecting mother, you too are carrying precious cargo. You are pregnant with purpose and destiny. Yes, destiny stretches you, keeps you up at night and it will take you out of your comfort zone. However, despite the pain, it's worth every tear you've had to cry to see it come to pass. God is just as vested in this pregnancy as you are, because you are carrying His promise. To ensure that His promise comes to pass, Jeremiah 1:12(Amp) states, "for I am [actively] watching over My word to fulfill it." You're not a single mom during this pregnancy. God is a great Father and He is there every step, ensuring that it will come to pass.

Our Focus Passage

Romans 4:20-21 (NIV)
Yet he did not waver through unbelief regarding the promise of God, but was strengthened in his faith and gave glory to God, being fully persuaded that God had power to do what he had promised.

Let's talk about it.

Our focus passage is speaking about Abraham, the father of faith. He had a promise from God and he believed that it would come to pass. He had to overcome his age, the physical impossibilities and doubt but in the end, Sarah gave birth to the promise. To others it would appear that they were the most unlikely candidates for the job, but God chose them. Maybe you are still scratching your head, wondering why the Lord hasn't given up on you, and He keeps reminding you of who you are, and of His promises. When others count you out, God counts you in. He specializes in the underdog. Your suffering was not in vain, but merely the labor pains to help birth the promise. His promise doesn't guarantee that you won't have complications, but that it will come to pass. God explains it in Psalms 34:19: "The righteous person may have many troubles, but the LORD delivers him from them all." So no matter what complications you experience during this pregnancy, He will deliver you out of all of them.

Carrying the promise requires a different environment and diet; you will have to stop eating junk food and avoid harmful environments. In other words, you can't let anyone speak doubt into your life or eat the words of negative people. As stated in Philippians 4:8 (NIV), "...whatever is true, whatever is noble, whatever is right, whatever is pure, whatever is lovely, whatever is admirable - if anything is excellent or praiseworthy - think about such things." Your environment must be pure, refusing to entertain gossip, keep up strife, or pettiness as the promise depends on it. You will have to sacrifice the things you want to do over the things you need to do, but it will be worth it. You might find yourself having second thoughts regarding carrying the promise, just as Sarah and Abraham did. However, God's response to your doubt is found in Genesis 18:14 (NIV): "Is anything too hard for the LORD? " There is nothing too hard for the Lord, and what you have to endure is worth every tear. Keep pushing, keep believing, and never doubt, but become "fully persuaded that God had power to do what he had promised" (Romans 4:21). It will surely come to pass!

Reflections:

- You have to guard your promise, as an expectant mother would protect her child. Think on positive things and remove the negative words, people, and actions out of your life.
- You are not alone; God is with you during this process and He promises to watch over you and His word to ensure that it comes to pass.

Your "GO" Challenge:

In your *Capture the Moment Journal*, make a list of what's in your environment that can be harmful to the promises, and how can you change it, e.g. negative people, habits, or lack of self-discipline.

The promise you carry is high-risk and all precaution must be taken. What do you need to add to your spiritual diet and environment to nurture the promise?

Confession:

My promise will come to pass! I am not defeated but I am fully persuaded that God will bring it to pass. I will not let my lack of resources or understanding detour me, but I will remain focused while relying on Jesus every step of the way. Lord, if You have to stretch me or if it requires me to carry more than I think I can bear, I trust You to help me. It is worth it. I will not abort the promise because of the thoughts and opinions of others. I will remove the negative habits, words and people that are harmful to my promise. It is worth it and the promise will speak and shall not lie. It will come to pass.

Day 27

—

Upgraded To A Crown Of Beauty

Everyone has a story. Regardless of their background or upbringing, no one's life reads the same. Some proudly tell their story while others hide in shame. Those who had a rough upbringing are expected to have troubles and setbacks. However, no one considers the one who was captain of the cheer team, most likely to succeed, and graduate from UCLA Medical School would have a story of humiliation and regret. 2 Samuel 13 records the story of Tamar; Absalom's sister, daughter of the beloved King David. She was a princess, living every woman's dream in the palace with servants, power and wealth. The Bible even speaks of how beautiful she was in 2 Samuel 13:1. However her storybook life would soon come to an end, and none of those things could save her. Her brother Ammon raped Tamar, and the princess who once roamed the kingdom with her head held high was openly disgraced. In 2 Samuel 13:19 records her tearing her royal robe and sprinkling ashes on her head. Those ashes represent a crown of shame as Tamar had lost hope of ever being restored.

Beloved, regardless of your story, whether rich or poor, raised by both parents or by none, married or single, God has still yet to write the next chapter in your book of life. The title of this new chapter is called, *"Upgraded to a Crown of Beauty."* Through the grace of God, your crown of shame has been removed and replaced with beauty. No longer will you hold your head down in disgrace; you are a queen.

Our Focus Passage

Isaiah 61:3 (NIV)

"...crown of beauty instead of ashes, the oil of joy instead of mourning, and a garment of praise instead of a spirit of despair."

Let's talk about it.

Ashes come from something that had been destroyed by fire on the altar. Life and hope was burned up, and all that was left were the ashes. This is what you assumed after all the devastation you have been through. Your plans, dreams, and aspirations were destroyed in the fire of life, and all you have left are the ashes of what used to be. It wasn't supposed to end like this. You made the right choices, so you never thought they would diagnose you with cancer. You gave your child the finest schooling and ensured they had nothing but the best, and yet he ended up on drugs. Although you may be covered in ashes, the Holy Spirit wants you to know that He is getting ready to make an upgrade to your crown. He is exchanging your crown of shame into one of beauty and He's turning the most dark and ugly parts of your life into a brilliant masterpiece. Where mourning and weeping dwelled, the Lord will cause the oil of joy to flow continuously in your house. You will have joy like a river that overflows into every area of your life.

In the book of Esther, chapter 4, Mordecai honored God and refused to bow and pay homage to Haman. In return he did not receive goodness but was met with a decree of death, which was a plot to kill him and the entire nation of Israel. The Bible states that "he tore his clothes, put on sackcloth and ashes" Esther 4:1. Not everything you are going through is your fault; sometimes, bad things happen to good people. However, God uses these situations to vindicate his people. You were serving God, and you were faithful and kind to those in need and was rewarded with death, depression, and suffering.

What you did not know is that the Lord has been preparing a feast for you in the presence of your enemies. The people or situations that fought you will have to turn around and honor you. In Esther Chapter 8, Mordecai is at the table with his enemy Haman. The King gave Mordecai his signet ring and he was awarded Haman's estate. Esther 8:15 (NIV) speaks of the upgrade he received: "When Mordecai left the king's presence, he was wearing royal garments of blue and white, a large crown of gold and a purple robe of fine linen." After the table has been set in your life, God will make the big announcement that you are no longer broken and distraught, wearing a crown of shame. The Lord has given you a crown of beauty and a new garment of praise. You have been upgraded to a crown of beauty for your ashes.

Reflections:
- There is an exchange that God is making in your life. He will right the wrongs and change your perspective on the situation.
- You have been upgraded and the crown of frustration and grief has been removed. You have received a crown of victory, peace and beauty.

Your "GO" Challenge:

Look in the mirror and, by faith, remove the crown of despair, sorrow, frustration, doubt, and anything that is beneath your privilege as a child of the King. Now, by faith, put on the crown of promise and purpose.

Confession:

I will not hold my head down in shame or defeat. I am royalty and a child of the King of kings. I remove any other crown placed on my head to denounce who I am in Christ. I thank God for upgraded emotion, finances, peace, and health.

Day 28

—

Nevertheless

In high school you had your life all planned out. You knew the career you would pursue; you even had your dream car and house picked out. Your faith went unchallenged and your dreams were limitless back then. However, while crossing over into adulthood reality overpowered your dreams and you started doing the things that you promised yourself you would never do. Jesus himself asked God to remove the burden he carried in Matthew 26:39. It's not the question of *"Why me?"* that is harmful, it is acting on it. Jesus could have refused to die, and abandon us, but He denied Himself so that others might gain eternal life.

Beloved, emotions are an important part of life, however it is how you act on those emotions that determine the outcome. Although Jesus asked God could the vision come to pass without suffering, He did not act on emotions. His confession was, *"Nevertheless!!"* While going through personal hardship, you must follow Christ's example and confess, "nevertheless not as I will but as thou wilt" Matthew 26:39 (KJV). That "nevertheless" allowed Jesus to die and rise with all power in His hand. Your "nevertheless" will also unlock the unlimited power needed to overcome the darkness and bring you into the light of his favor and glory.

Our Focus Passage
Philippians 4:12-13 (NIV)
I know what it is to be in need, and I know what it is to have plenty. I have learned the secret of being content in any and every situation, whether well fed or hungry, whether living in plenty or in want. I can do all this through him who gives me strength.

Let's talk about it.

Everyone wants the blessings and prosperity of God, but no one would willingly sign up to go through hardship and pain. All the trials and tribulations are for the glory that is going to be revealed in your life. The tears and the pain you endure behind closed doors produce the glory and favor that shines on the outside. It's not a coincidence that you don't look like what you've been through. In Daniel 3:27 (KJV), after the three Hebrew boys came out of the fire it states: "...upon whose bodies the fire had no power, nor was a hair of their head singed, neither were their coats changed, nor the smell of fire had passed on them." Not only will God deliver you from the fiery trials of life; you won't smell like, look like, or be affected by what you just endured. When you say "nevertheless" to God, His grace will change the outcome of a situation that should have destroyed you.

The three Hebrew boys, Shadrach, Meshach and Abed-nego, were doing what was right in the eyes of God; which caused them to encounter hardship. Often, we feel as if we have done something wrong and this why we're going through difficult times. However, that is not always the case. This time it is your yes to God that got you into this mess, and your yes will get you out. Some will say, "I am tired of going through struggles; I will just settle on blending in." However, the blood of Jesus has marked you.

Remember that you can do all things; which sometimes includes enduring good times as well as the bad. Your "nevertheless" will cause the Son of the Living God to get off the throne and come and attend to your needs. Notice in the story of the three Hebrew boys that God did not rescue them from the fire but gave them power to withstand and conquer it. God's methods are confusing and hard for the human mind to understand. Yet, when you don't understand his method, trust his heart. He loves you more than any human relationship you have experienced. When you say yes, he says yes: yes to deliverance, healing, and to being made whole.

Reflections:
- You have good times and will have to endure hard times, but through it all God is with you and has given you the power to overcome. All He requires is a yes.
- God's methods don't always make sense; so when you don't trust his methods, trust His heart for He loves you.

Your "GO" Challenge:

Look into a mirror and tell yourself, your emotions, your will, and your mind, *"Nevertheless! I am going to endure and conquer this and God, I trust your heart."*

In your **Capture the Moment Journal**, make a list of the top three things you need to say "Nevertheless" to:

Confession:

Lord I trust you. I know I don't always understand, but I believe Your words. You said You will never put more on me than I can bear, and when the load gets heavy You told me to cast it upon You. I'm not where I want to be, but I am further along than where I used to be. I am growing in grace and overcoming every day. I own this day and declare that I have victory; and when the fire gets turned up in my life I will not abort my purpose to get rid of the pain. I will endure, and I will survive; I will come out victorious.

Day 29

—

I Will Encourage Myself

When God created the heavens and the earth, after each creation day He celebrated His accomplishments by looking at what He created and calling it good. Once He completed His work He paused to admire His creation again. Genesis 1:31 (NIV) states: "God saw all that he had made, and it was very good…"

Accomplishments are important, whether big or small. God took the moment to celebrate after each creation day, and once everything was finished He celebrated again. You have come a long way in your journey of faith and wholeness. However, how often do you take a moment to celebrate the milestones in your life? It's easy to get discouraged because it seems as if you are making little to no progress. However, this could not be further from the truth. You are making progress; you just haven't stopped to celebrate them.

You've decided to start doing or stop doing something that puts you closer to your breakthrough. Although it might not be worthy of a tweet or Facebook update, it is progress. We often want to wait for total completion before we feel it's worthy of celebration. However, our Creator demonstrates how one should handle each step of progress. I am not saying you should plan a banquet, but go and treat yourself to a massage for enrolling back in school, or for applying for the promotion. King David, the man after God's own heart, had to do the same thing in 1 Samuel 30:6. It states, "…but David encouraged himself in the Lord his God." Beloved, when others can't see your efforts or appreciate your sacrifice, get up and declare, *"I will encourage myself in the Lord."*

Our Focus Passage

Joshua 1:9 (NIV)

Have I not commanded you? Be strong and courageous. Do not be afraid; do not be discouraged, for the LORD your God will be with you wherever you go."

Let's talk about it.

Could you imagine going to a playoff game and nobody cheered, not even the fans? The players would lose heart and the excitement of winning would be lost. This is true in your life; each touchdown or yards gained must be celebrated. In this season of your life, God is focused on the yards you've gained and celebrates them. There was a time you watered the promise with the tears you cried. Now it is your season to celebrate! It's time to celebrate the growth of your harvest, as the deliverance and promise of peace is springing forth.

Take a moment to reflect: you and your spouse are speaking now without it turning into an argument, or you woke up feeling productive instead of depressed. Look at your accomplishments, and like God did in the beginning, say, *"They are good!"*

In the focus passage, God tells Joshua, "Do not be afraid; do not be discouraged." He tells Joshua this because there will be days when situations or people will attempt to beat you down. When those moments come, you have to be your own cheerleader and tell yourself to keep going and to be of good courage.

There will be days when you don't feel it but you know that everything is working out for your good. Our focus passage Joshua 1:9 (NIV) explains why you can be strong and have courage: "...for the LORD your God will be with you wherever you go." if you have a day where you are depressed, God is there, or if you park your attitude in the driveway of defeat, God is there. David said it best in Psalms 139:8 (NKJV): "If I ascend into heaven, you are there; If I make my bed in hell, behold, you are there." No matter where you find yourself in life, the Lord is there, commanding you to be strong and be of good courage.

Reflections:

- Through the ups and downs in life God has commanded you to be encouraged, not because all is well, but because He is with you.
- Learn to celebrate the accomplishments in your life as you have gained yards and you are one step closer to your promise.
- Don't fear what the day may bring, for God is with you and it is His job to protect and care for you.

Your "GO" Challenge:

This week take a moment to celebrate your milestones in life, no matter how big or small. Log them in your Capture the Moment journal. Log the dates, and as time passes, watch the progress unfold.

Confession:

I am making progress I am moving forward. I will celebrate my accomplishments because I am proud of me and so is God. I will continue to strive until I see my promise come to pass. I will not wait for others to approve of me, because God's approval is more than enough. I will focus on the yards gained in life, and get over what I thought was a loss. I am wiser and understand that although I don't always feel like it, God is there, cheering me on. He tells me not to be afraid, so I won't; I will be strong and courageous.

Day 30

—

Lost In His Presence

There comes a moment in life when you can get lost in His presence. Nothing else matters, and the noise is muffled out by the pure peace of God. It's a peace that makes the storms of life be still and the worries cease. The Lord states in Proverbs 18:10 (NIV), "The name of the LORD is a strong fortress; the godly run to him and are safe." His presence will keep you and shield you from the storm. The fortress was a place in the kingdom where you could go if you were under attack. It was made of thick walls and heavily fortified by the military guard. Those who had access to this fortress could escape the battle and never have to engage in war.

Beloved, you have strained, fought and toiled long enough. It is time for you to get into the fortress of His presence. It is time to get lost in His presence and leave the fighting to him. When you take refuge in his presence He makes a commitment to hide and keep you safe. Psalms 31:20 (NLT): "You hide them in the shelter of your presence, safe from those who conspire against them. You shelter them in your presence, far from accusing tongues." Those situations you have tried to fix and mend were not meant for you to fight but to hide in the presence of God.

Our Focus Passage
Psalms 91:1 (NKJV)
He that dwelleth in the secret place of the Most High shall abide under the shadow of the Almighty.

Let's talk about it.

There are benefits that come with being in God's presence. God has prepared a place where we can go and escape the cares of this world. Heaven is the ultimate place, but He desires His children to have access to Him on demand. If you need joy you will find it in His presence. Psalms 16:11 (KJV) states, "Thou wilt shew me the path of life: in thy presence is fullness of joy; at thy right hand, there are pleasures for evermore." In his presence your joy will never go empty, and there you will find directions and clarity.

Unfortunately, the presence of the Lord is usually the last place we seek when we are in trouble. We call on our friends, and we will exhaust our resources before we realize that nothing is working. He doesn't want to be the last resort, but the only source. Psalms 32:7 states, "You are my hiding place; you will protect me from trouble and surround me with songs of deliverance." If it seems as if the enemy is attacking you at every turn, perhaps you are making it too easy for him to find you. Hiding in God's presence not only keeps you safe, as the enemy cannot attack what he cannot see. As a Christian, there are many ways to war in the spirit, such as fasting, praise and worship, and prayer. We never consider hiding from our enemy in the presence of the Lord.

You're not hiding because you are afraid to fight; you are hiding because you don't have to fight. David was a mighty warrior with the ability to defeat Saul; however, God wanted David to rest and trust in Him. Exodus 14:14 says, "The LORD will fight for you; you need only to be still." What God is saying is come and hide in me and be still, so that troubles can't find you. You can't argue your way out, reason your way out, or plead your way. You will have to hide your way out of this one. It is during those quiet and still moments in His presence that He restores your peace, joy, and strength. Turn off the T.V., power off your phones and create an atmosphere of worship and praise for Him to inhabit. Once He shows up, don't rush to bombard Him with requests. Be still and allow Him to minister and mend every hurting and dry space in your life as you abide in the secret place of the almighty God.

Reflections:

- There is a place in God where you can go where troubles and worry cannot find you.
- It was not meant for you to fight every battle. Hiding in his presence doesn't mean you can't fight; it just means you don't have to, because The Lord will fight for you.
- You cannot argue your way out of this or use your own strength to deliver yourself. However, His Spirit can deliver you, says the Lord.

Your "GO" Challenge:

In your *Capture the Moment Journal*, make a list of the distractions you need to remove.

Then, schedule your divine appointment to hide in God's presence. Set aside 1 hour out of your day where you turn off social media, television and any other distraction. Allow you and God to be alone and uninterrupted. Create an environment fit for a King; play worship music and just begin to give God thanks and praise. Begin to meditate on what the Spirit of the Lord is saying to you in that very moment.

Confession:

Lord, I will put down my weapons and hide in Your presence. I will be still, awaiting Your instructions for my life. I don't have to fight the battle, but I will rest in You. I will not be consumed by the cares of this world but I will remain in Your presence, while allowing You to strengthen me and make me whole. I will get lost in Your presence.

Made in the USA
San Bernardino, CA
10 July 2018